# Thumbs Up!

for *The Home Office Handbook: Rules of Thumb for Organizing Your Time, Information, and Workspace*

"As we manage our work+life fit, more of us will work and live in the same space, either on our own as an entrepreneur or remotely for someone else. The Home Office Handbook, by my go-to organizational guru Lorie Marrero, shows you how to create a home-based work environment that sets you up for personal and professional success.
Must read!"

*Cali Williams Yost, flexible work strategy expert and author of* **TWEAK IT: Make What Matter to You Happen Every Day**

"Even those of us who've never met a filing cabinet we liked will find tips in this handy book to keep the home office organized and make the most of our time. Lorie is practical and cheers all improvements without insisting you do anything that won't work with your life."

*Laura Vanderkam, author of* **What the Most Successful People Do Before Breakfast**, *and* **168 Hours**

"Being organized is critical to growing your business fast. Lorie's book delivers specific actions you can apply immediately to get organized and stay there. This book is a must-read if you're ready to take your business to the next level."

*Jason Dorsey, bestselling author,* **Y-Size Your Business**

Reason
Press

Reason Press
PO Box 40460
Austin, TX 78704
512-498-9800
publisher@reasonpresspublishing.com

**Published by Reason Press in conjunction with River Grove Books, a division of Greenleaf Book Group LLC.**

First Edition
ISBN 978-0-9826090-2-6

Images used by license from Shutterstock.com and iStockphoto.com unless otherwise specified.

*"Far and away the best prize that life has to offer is the chance to work hard at work worth doing."*

-Theodore Roosevelt

This book is dedicated to my friends and partners at Goodwill Industries International®, who believe in *the power of work,* and the program participants who inspire me every single day. Learn how your donations turn into jobs at ***donate.goodwill.org***.

# TABLE OF CONTENTS

# GET STARTED

Hello, friend!

Before we get to the "good part," let's go over the very practical matter of how to get the most from this book.

## Print Your Note-Taking Guide

If you are reading this book, you probably are wishing for more time to be available for your work and life, and I am honored that you are investing your time reading my advice.

> **To make sure that your time investment is best leveraged, please go to** *clutterdiet.com/homeofficenotes* **to print a PDF note-taking guide** I have created for you to centralize the ACTIONS you are going to take after reading. Otherwise, life will continue to get in the way, and you'll soon forget what you wanted to put into practice! No personal information or sign-up is required-- the link takes you to the actual file.

## Watch Me Show You How

Throughout this book we'll refer to the exclusive bonus video tutorials I made just for YOU, the purchasers of this book! All of those tutorials are available to you at **clutterdiet.com/homeofficevideos.**

## Why the Home Office?

**We are in the Golden Age of Home Offices!** In times past, we needed only papers and pens and a few office supplies to pay our personal bills. Now with computers and printers we have all needed to carve out a space in our homes to locate our administrative tasks for the everyday needs of any family.

Many homes have a dedicated home office, even if nobody is running a business. And more of us than ever are able to earn a living from home in various ways, whether we are telecommuting full- or part-time or operating our own entrepreneurial ventures.

**Home offices have unique challenges and benefits, especially if you are earning your money from your own living space.** While it's true that you can work in your pajamas, you have a 25-foot commute, you have increased flexibility with your personal obligations, and you get some decent tax deductions, you also may have trouble closing up shop and finding balance.

I have been a Professional Organizer since 2000, working with clients in their home offices as well as working in my own home office. I have seen two or three full time employees share space in a client's home every working day, I have seen people working solo 100% of the time, and I have personally had employees and contractors coming into my own home off and on for years.

**While I have a great deal of experience organizing for corporate clients in formal office settings, my heart belongs to the home office.** I was moved to take what I have learned and pour it into a handbook to help people better enjoy working in their living spaces. Let's work together to get a grip on our work and have more fun!

## The Most Important Question of All

As we get started, the most important question I can possibly ask you is this:

| WHY are you reading this book? |
| :---: |

I would like you to take a moment and reflect upon this question, because **if you don't have a compelling reason to make changes in your life, to create good habits and end bad ones, let's be frank about it—you probably won't.**

Yes, you want more time, you want less stress… but so does everybody.

What is your deeper reason? **I know what it is.**

**I believe everyone is uniquely suited to CREATE.** It doesn't matter if you are "not a creative person" and don't know how to draw or paint. What you create could be a magnificent business. It could be the best cherry pie in the county, or a nurturing environment for children to thrive, or a book you want to write, or an inspiring speech you want to give. It could be a fruitful garden, a new charitable organization, or a service you want to provide.

**Creation is our life's work; it's what we are meant to do with our own two hands. Whatever that is for you, you're not getting enough of it or you wouldn't be reading this book.**

We all want more time and energy to be freed up so we can focus on what we really want to create, build, do, and enjoy.

**As an organizing expert, the purpose of *my* creations is to help you focus on your own.**

**I hope that you'll take a moment to make notes about your big WHY in your note-taking guide**, so that when things get out of hand, you'll be motivated to get a grip. **Humor me and write something down. (Get it at *clutterdiet.com/homeofficenotes*)**

## *I Think You Probably Should Be More Decisive*

**The origin of clutter is delayed decisions and delayed actions.** Think about that—everything you see on the countertops, on the floors, in your email inbox, and even the random thoughts floating around your brain as mental clutter—are all decisions unmade or actions untaken.

**Therefore, the root of clutter is PROCRASTINATION.** So let's stop putting off these decisions:

- What to keep

- Where to store it
- Where to donate it
- Whether to say yes
- When to do it
- What to do right now
- What to do next

**First, take ownership.** Someone needs to make the decisions—is it you? If not, could it be you? Issues have a way of lingering when nobody takes ownership of the problem. Even something as fun as deciding where to go on vacation never gets resolved when each party thinks the other person is going to decide. Time slips away and before you know it, flights are sold out. Have the important conversations that are necessary to determine ownership.

**Set goals and deadlines.** Commit to making the decisions. I am not joking when I tell people to throw a party to help themselves get organized! Something about the idea of people coming over to visit really motivates you to get busy on your organizing projects. It's a great way to set an artificial deadline. You may have a real one, like an upcoming move or the birth of a baby. Use the pressure to your advantage!

**Narrow your choices.** Having too many choices can be paralyzing, like facing the salsa aisle in an Austin supermarket. Maybe if you're deciding where to go on vacation, you could narrow your choices by saying you'll only travel within this hemisphere. If it's salsa, you could narrow it down to only green (verde) sauces, or just mild ones (if you're a wimp). Whenever possible in this book, I am going to teach you tools to help you limit your choices, like our Action-Reference-Trash method of sorting information.

**Be a "satisficer" not a "maximizer."** Author Barry Schwartz (*The Paradox of Choice: Why More is Less*) teaches about the work of 1950s psychologist Herbert Simon, who identified these two types of decision-makers.

A maximizer is someone who perfectionistically needs to be assured that every decision they make is the best possible, causing them to review every possible alternative. **Maximizers worry that there is always something better around the corner.**

**Satisficers are people who move forward without worrying about whether there is something better,** once they have found a decent option that meets their criteria and standards.

**Which one of these types are you?** If you can work on arresting your thought processes in the moment and steering yourself toward being a satisficer, you'll be more organized.

**Make "policies" to make the decisions easier.** If you set rules for yourself, they become the guiding force to make choices for you. You may decide, for example, that if you have magazines older than 3 months you will recycle them without reading them. Further, you might even set a rule that magazines stacked up over a certain number of months mean that you will unsubscribe to that publication.

**Usually indecisiveness is based in fear,** since it often means you are afraid of making "The Wrong Choice." What is the worst thing that could happen? Make a decision to work on your decisiveness. I think you'll be better organized and save time for other things. I am pretty sure.

## How to Get a Handle on It

**To get a grip on your home office, ideally take a block of time of at least half a day to completely focus on it.** Investing in setting up these systems is the best way to "sharpen the saw," as Stephen Covey says. Taking a small amount of time to optimize and maintain your tools means you will be more efficient. **Who is more effective, the guy with the dull saw blade who hacks away all day long, or the guy who takes breaks to sharpen his saw so it works better?**

A holiday or weekend day is best, if possible, to avoid interruptions. I am the first person to agree that everyone needs to rest and take breaks, and please do so. But if you have a three day weekend coming up, that's two days of rest and one of working on your home office.

Your note-taking guide will provide a plan of action for you. **If you can't get a block of time to work on these projects, at least pick a few new habits to add into your daily routines and keep looking for an opportunity to schedule that blocked time.**

**When you are spending concentrated time organizing your office,** *focus on sorting and scheduling.* "Doing" things, like calling the carpet cleaners when you locate that lost coupon or browsing through that catalog you just found, will distract you and you won't make progress!

Your task is to get everything sorted and into a system, and then take action on whatever you find once your systems are in place. **If there is something you need to do, you will write it on your task list or calendar and keep going with your sorting. Agreed?**

**As you sort through your piles and files, start with the most recent items first and work your way back.** This approach may seem counterintuitive if you have the intention of being very thorough, but usually what is older is no longer relevant. You can start using your systems more quickly if you build them around what you're currently thinking about and doing.

**If possible, trade favors with a friend to work with you.** She can, for example, work through your home office with you, and you can help her with her garage the next weekend. **You'll both benefit from two things you cannot possibly get by working alone: ACCOUNTABILITY and OBJECTIVITY.**

**There is no substitute for this incredibly valuable perspective of an objective other.** You have been looking at this stuff too long. You have emotional attachments and irrational blocks about many of the things sitting in your piles that only an objective person can point out to you. When someone hires a professional organizer, objectivity is one of the big needle-movers in the process, along with the experience and expertise we bring.

**Working with a friend gives you accountability by having an appointment to get it done.** You won't be able to rationalize procrastinating by doing other projects or activities instead on your own. **It's happening.** You're forced to focus.

**Your first assignment here is to set a date and choose a friend.** If a friend can't work with you in person, at least be accountable to someone for the time slot you've assigned yourself and report back to that person on your progress.

Get your note-taking guide at *clutterdiet.com/homeofficenotes* and write down what you've decided.

# Time + Choices

Let's get started with the biggest problems first. The most common complaint I hear is, "I don't have enough time." And second to that is hearing about problems with paper and information. **What most people don't realize is that time and information are connected like a hand and glove.**

**Your hand represents your time, focus and energy-- your work. And the glove represents the information you need to do your work--** all of your emails, letters, tutorials, magazines, surveys, instructions, spreadsheets, and other information in your life.

**What's key to recognize is that without the hand, the glove just sits there, lifeless. YOU bring information to life.** Your time, focus, and energy are required to create anything with it.

As you process a stack of paper, you will run across something in the pile that requires work from you. A phone call needs to be made. An errand needs to be done. A person needs to be hired. **Handling that information requires you to use the tools related to your time, focus, and energy, namely your calendar and task list. I have seen many people make the mistake of trying to process information without having these tools nearby or even set up in the first place.**

**So our hand-in-glove perspective on time and information helps us understand that in order to be more productive and effective, we have to look at these two issues of "time" and "information" together.** Like peanut butter and jelly, rice and beans, Batman and Robin.

So how do we find more time? We try to manage it. "Time Management," they call it. **Time management has often been taught as a one-size-fits-all approach**. If you just follow this person's system exactly, buy this specific kind of planner, or use this software, you'll be successful!

Ladies and gentlemen, that is "old school." Yes, there are some basic concepts and we are going to cover them here, but **I believe your style of managing your time is as unique as your fingerprint.**

Everyone has different demands, different values, different experiences, and different brains. **We need to have the flexibility to change our systems when our needs change, and some of us simply need variety and novelty to stay engaged. Some of us are very comfortable in a digital world, and some of us need paper to feel in control.** The leather-bound day planner you used before may not work for you as well as a smartphone calendar does now, and you might prefer a sticky note of daily tasks while another person needs all of it in Outlook.

**"Time Management" is also a bit of a misnomer.** No matter how powerful we are in this world, we all have the same 168 hours in a week, and time marches on, second-by-second… we can manage our relationship to it, but time itself is not controllable.

**Time is simply one of our resources. What we absolutely can manage are *our choices* in any given moment.**

**So instead of "Time Management," think of it instead as "Choice Management."**

> TIME IS A CREATED THING. TO SAY, "I DON'T HAVE TIME," IS TO SAY, "I DON'T WANT TO."
> - Lao Tzu

Our choices are dictated by mainly four things:

- ✓ **Our priorities:** We may have the highest motives for the day, but if a child gets sick or a computer problem happens, our priorities shift in an instant. Our priorities are mostly determined by our personal values.
- ✓ **Our focus:** We are more distracted than ever, with social media and mobile technology ever-present and the expectation of instant response.

✓ **Our resources:** When we choose how to spend any given Monday morning, we are situationally dependent upon the availability of energy, technology, money, tools, and time. We probably cannot work on a laptop efficiently if we are standing in line at the DMV. And we cannot use our brains and bodies efficiently if we've not had the right nutrition and rest.

✓ **Our culture:** We don't exist in a vacuum. We exist within a family or a company or a country or a network of some kind, and the culture around us dictates what expectations we have of ourselves and others. Expectations in areas like punctuality, responsiveness, courtesy, service, and attitude overlay our daily interactions. With today's technology, "urgent" no longer means costly and special-- it's free and ubiquitous and *expected*. Culture change is possible, but usually it takes deliberate effort.

## *Your Choice Management Fingerprint*

So we're going to move beyond the term "time management" and focus on how to create a system to help us manage our choices based on our priorities, focus, resources, culture… and information.

I believe successful choice management involves these 5 components, and they are flexible and are determined by your personal preferences and circumstances:

**CAPTURE:** The tools and practices you use to capture information

**COMMIT:** The filtering of your captured information to make choices

**CUE:** The tools and practices that prompt you to take actions at the right time

**COMPLETE:** Accomplishing your committed actions

**CORRECT:** Reviewing tools and systems and evaluating your choices

## Capture

Information is flying at us from all directions, from our computer screens and mailboxes to the ads on the side of a bus. **Our busy brains cannot be trusted to remember everything on their own, so we need tools to help us grab and hold ideas securely until we can make choices and put them into our systems… or not.** We may decide the information we capture does not fit into our plans, and we mostly filter through it and discard it in our next step. **Some things are just obvious and we put them directly into our systems, like a haircut appointment or note to pick up a gift for a birthday.**

**The more you try to keep things in your head, the more stress you will feel.** Capturing is a discipline, a practice. Effort is required to stop and capture something, and it's tempting to try keeping it in our heads. But consider what I call "The Bookmark Principle." The lowly bookmark is one of the best, most simple capturing tools. Is it smarter to use a bookmark or to go around everywhere chanting inside your head, "I'm on page 13, I'm on page 13, I'm on page 13…"? Using a bookmark captures that information so that our brainpower can be free to work on more important tasks. **Imagine relying upon your trusty capturing tools for everything, just like you rely on a bookmark! How much more brainpower will you have available to be productive and happy?**

Our personal preferences will dictate our favorite capturing tools. Choose a few tools from this menu of options, or add your own favorites that already work for you, and write them down in your note-taking guide. Keep in mind where you typically are and what you're typically doing as you capture information. Most people need to have options for both at home and away.

### FOR IDEAS:

- ☑ **Paper and pen:** best to have a consistent notebook you use both at and away from your desk.

- ☑ **Email:** sending a message to yourself while out or having others email you.

☑ **Evernote:** for laptop, smartphone, & tablet—I have exclusive video training for you on this on your tutorials page at *clutterdiet.com/homeofficevideos*, and you can read about that in a later section. Grab any image, take a photo of something, paste something from the web, save an article from an email, etc. and tag and it search for it whenever you need it. *www.evernote.com*

☑ **ReQall:** better than calling yourself and leaving a voicemail message-- you call, speak your message recording, and you receive a transcribed email minutes later of what you said. Perfect for ideas that occur while driving, can be used from any kind of phone, and it's FREE. You can watch me demonstrate ReQall on your video tutorials page, at *clutterdiet.com/homeofficevideos*. *www.reqall.com/app*

☑ **Camera:** Take photos of things like the parking lot sign where you parked your car or the hours of operation for a business. Take photos of articles or recipes you find in a waiting room magazine. (If you use Evernote, use the camera function within it to create a new note with that photo.)

☑ **SnagIt:** I use this software every single day and have shown it to many friends, clients and vendors who love it too. It takes screen captures of particular regions of the screen, scrolling windows, or whatever you need, with sophisticated features like optional time delays so you can pull down a menu if needed… then it puts the screenshot into an easy editor where you can circle things, add notes, arrows, and callouts, and easily copy or save to send to others or paste into another application (like Evernote or a document). You can also do a simple video capture of your screen for a process or sequence of something. Fantastic! *www.techsmith.com/snagit.html*

☑ **Inbox:** A tray in your kitchen, your office, or wherever is convenient for you to gather and corral any mail or other physical items that need sorting. Also can think of this as your "To Be Sorted" basket.

☑ **Printed Material:** Grab the magazine article you're reading or the brochure or the handout that is provided at a meeting and put it in your inbox to process.

✓ **Objects:** Put a gadget that needs repairs into your inbox to physically capture the idea that you need to fix it. Put a training DVD into your inbox to capture it until you remember to schedule a time to watch it.

✓ **Sorting folder:** Designate a folder or pouch to have with you on the road, in a briefcase or other bag, which operates as your inbox while you are away. When you get back, put these items into your normal inbox to process.

# FOR APPOINTMENTS:

✓ **Ring-bound planner:** traditional planners, such as those from Franklin Covey, with removable pages, weekly views, monthly views, and daily view pages along with contact information and other modules.

✓ **Spiral planner:** products like Planner Pad and Mom Agenda, which are more streamlined than larger planners.

✓ **Pocket planner:** smaller calendars for purses or pockets, like Whomi, WeekDate, and others.

✓ **Wall calendar:** good for sharing information about family activities and getting a view from around the room. I don't recommend wipe-off versions of these, as the history is not preserved.

✓ **Microsoft Outlook:** my calendar of choice, as it is so widely used and powerful.

✓ **Google Calendar:** in the cloud, easily shared, synchronizes easily with Android phones.

✓ **iCal:** Apple's calendar application, synchronizes easily with iPhones.

✓ **Smartphones:** your phone's own calendar, dozens of calendar apps, or synchronization with the cloud or desktop for Outlook, Google, or iCal.

## FOR TASKS:

☑ **Notebook:** Moleskines, Arc notebooks from Staples, Circa notebooks from Levenger, any spiral notebook from any store.

☑ **Notepad:** Legal pads, any pad of any kind of paper you like, but be consistent.

☑ **Smartphone apps:** RememberTheMilk, ToodleDo, Any.Do, built-in phone apps.

☑ **Microsoft Outlook:** Great choice if you use the calendar and email functions.

☑ **Reminders:** Apple's option with iCal/iPhone.

☑ **ReQall:** Call in to capture a task into your system.

☑ **Desktop or web applications:** Workflowy, RememberTheMilk, ToodleDo or Evernote.

**From the Capturing tools you chose, choose a Primary Calendar and a Primary Task List.** These are your basic Commitment tools you'll use in the next step, and typically these are the tools you'll use when you're working at your desk. (For me, they are Microsoft Outlook, for both calendar and task list.) Write those down on your note-taking guide. (*clutterdiet.com/homeofficenotes*)

## Commit

You're cruising around capturing things, and at some point you need to process this information and make decisions about it. This step is where the hand meets the glove... you are deciding which information to use toward your objectives and committing to it in your calendar and task list.

**You will need to have regular times when you process this information, daily, weekly, and at other intervals** depending upon your particular needs.

There is not a magic formula for how often to process your information, because every situation is different. **But for most people who are trying to be productive with work five or six days a week, here is a suggestion:**

## DAILY:

☑ Process email at least once, ideally getting to your Happy Number each day (There is a difference between processing and checking! See the Email chapter where we get into much more detail and explain Happy Numbers).

☑ Process incoming paper mail, or at least get everything corralled in the inbox to be sorted.

☑ Review your calendar and task list at the beginning of the day, and again at the end of the day for tomorrow if possible.

## WEEKLY:

☑ Process your physical inbox completely until it is empty.

☑ Process your email inbox until you reach your Happy Number (see Email section to find out what this means).

☑ Review your calendar and task list with the previous, current, and next weeks in mind. Anything you need to follow up on from last week? Anything happen this week that needs more consideration? What's coming up next week?

☑ Process all of your capturing tools to make decisions on what's there.

**Our next chapter on Processing Information provides you a thorough and detailed guide on exactly how to process all of your captured items, with a flowchart of how to think through each step of your choice management.** Right now let's stay high-level and go through all of the steps.

So if Capturing is the "what," then Committing is the "who, why, when, where, and how."

✓ **WHY should this action be done or this information be kept?** Does it align with your goals and priorities? Many captured items will stop right here, as it does not make sense to take action on them. The information may not require any action at all, in which case you can file it away or discard it.

✓ **WHO should do this?** Can you delegate or outsource this action?

✓ **WHEN should it get done?** Is there a natural deadline, or do you need to create one? Is this something you can defer until later?

✓ **HOW should it get done?** Do you need to have an appointment on the calendar, or just list it on your task list? Do you need to arrange a meeting with someone else? Do you need to be accountable to someone to get it done? Are there any special tools or additional information needed to get it done?

✓ **WHERE should it get done?** At your desk, on the road, in a conference room?

If you're going to take action on something, you'll decide at this point whether you will *Handle It Now*, *Handle It Later*, or *Hand It Off*. We'll talk more about this later in Processing Information.

**When you Commit to an action, you will have your own personal ways of signifying that commitment.** You may simply put it on your calendar, put it on a master task list, move it up in a list, highlight it in a list or put a star next to it, put it on a sticky note, or start a folder to collect related information for a larger project. **I cannot**  **emphasize enough that you must do what works for you and your brain and your circumstances...** don't feel like you must adopt someone else's prescribed system and do it perfectly.

**Fridays are a great day to process things on a weekly basis**, since you're closing one week and preparing for another, and Fridays are commonly a little slower in pace for many people. Many people function best by making an appointment with themselves for this weekly processing time so that it doesn't get pushed aside.

**Ultimately, Committing to tasks, projects and appointments is most effective when you have clarity on your purpose, your goals, and your responsibilities.** You make much better decisions about priorities when you understand what you are working toward and why. And your Committed items may change from day-to-day, moment-to-moment, as "life happens"-- you may get that emergency phone call that shifts everything. That is okay, as long as it's a true emergency and you're not just getting meaninglessly sidetracked. If you're clear on your purpose and goals, it makes those things easier to discern. As novelist Tom Robbins said, "Stay committed to your decisions, but stay flexible in your approach."

## Cue

Anything you Commit to needs to have an accompanying reminder to make sure you get it done. Life moves pretty fast, and you want to make sure you are not going to forget what you have decided is important.

**Ask yourself, "WHAT'S MY CUE?" on a constant basis!** Don't rely on your memory alone. Take it from me, as the years go by this gets less and less reliable…

**I use my calendar for a regular Cue and check it daily.** I also use reminder alarms on Outlook and my smartphone. Members of our Clutter Diet program can use our customized e-mail reminder system to send themselves messages at any kind of repeating interval (weekly, every other day, every 3rd month, etc.).

**If you really must use your short-term memory to capture some information, you can use an object to help you remember that you are remembering.** Sometimes I keep something in my mind and move a ring to a different, more awkward finger so I will remember to capture it in a more permanent way as soon as possible.

**Here are the factors that make your CUES work,** whether they are Outlook/smartphone alarms, sticky notes, or wake-up calls:

- ☑ **Takes the burden off memory.** Don't worry your pretty little head about miniscule details, let your choice management system do it for you! Reduces stress and avoids mistakes.

- ☑ **Placed in an unavoidable path.** Think of your Future Self and figure out how to trick him/her into seeing the message no matter what. Example: putting your keys with your lunch in the refrigerator so you can't forget your lunch on the way to work.

- ☑ **Absolutely noticeable.** Your cues must have the element of novelty that allows your brain to notice things. Novelties might include color, interruption, sound, or placement. Otherwise Cues become like wallpaper and your eyes just gloss over them. (Got sticky notes on your monitor that have been there for a while?)

- ☑ **Appears exactly at the right time.** You can't have a reminder that then puts the burden back on memory because it's too soon before it was needed.

- ☑ **BONUS FACTOR: Being humorous and surprising.** If you can creatively put humor and surprise into the mix, it anchors the thoughts in your mind and makes them into stronger impressions. One summer my sons were leaving the garage with their bikes without shutting the garage door. I put a colorful sticky note on the back door that said "Shut the garage door." And that worked for a day, but it quit working because they would go in the garage from that door, get the bikes all ready, and then the Cue wasn't there at the right time. So I took some sidewalk chalk and I wrote right on the driveway, "Shut the garage door" in large letters so they could not avoid it. This Cue was humorous and surprising and it worked. You don't always have to be that creative, but keep in mind that the novelty sometimes is a factor with a good Cue.

Choose the reminder methods that you know work best for you based on the type of tools you've chosen and write those into your note-taking guide.

## *Complete*

So now you've Captured your information, you've Committed to doing it by making an appointment on your calendar or putting it on your task list, and you've been reminded to do it by your brilliant system of Cues. **All you have now is to DO THE WORK--** Complete the tasks. That's not so hard, right?

**Okay, it is hard. Let's be honest.** Your reminder cued you to take action and you just don't wanna. Most of us do procrastinate! And staying focused is no picnic either.

**I think Socrates said it best when he said, "Know Thyself." If you understand what motivates you to take action, that understanding is probably the biggest factor of all.** Rewards are a great motivator, and sometimes fear and consequences are very effective too! For me, I work best with deadlines and accountability to others, and I think that is true for most people.

**There are three key factors that compel people to take action:**

- ☑ **It's ESSENTIAL.** If you don't do it, something will explode or someone will suffer. Customers won't get their orders, for example, or kids won't be able to attend school. Completing these tasks is not as difficult because your motivation is very high to cross these urgent and important things off your list.

- ☑ **It's EVIDENT.** You will do things more easily if they are internally motivating to you. You're going to brush your teeth every day because you want to have fresh breath and healthy gums. You might eat more healthfully because you're motivated internally to feel better and take better care of yourself. You personally value the outcome because it aligns with who you are and who you want to become, and you build practices around these tasks.

☑ **It's EXTERNALLY MOTIVATED.** The task is difficult to complete, but you are accountable to someone or something else. Often this means deadlines, consequences, and/or rewards. Maybe you will be getting an evaluation from your manager, or a big bonus. **If you're having trouble completing something, usually you need more external motivation.** How can you achieve that? I believe accountability is the cure. I get most big things done by answering to my two longtime Accountability Partners. I wrote this eBook and my first book (*The Clutter Diet*) by getting up at 5:00AM every day and emailing them, "I'm up." Even if you are internally motivated for the bigger idea, sometimes the daily chunks of activity required to achieve it require something outside yourself to push you forward. Go to your bonus tutorials page online at *clutterdiet.com/homeofficevideos* to see a lesson from me on how to set up an Accountability Partnership.

**Finally, you can consider another letter E, and that is "ELIMINATE."** If you're not getting it done, maybe it really doesn't align with your goals. And maybe it's something that isn't as urgent as you thought. And sometimes that's what works. You just cross it off the list and move forward.

**Distraction is the biggest nemesis for many of us trying to Complete our Committed tasks.** Shutting extra windows on your computer, turning off your wireless internet access using airplane mode or a "kill" switch on your laptop, and turning off unnecessary alerts are very needed weapons against this adversary. I love what Tony Schwartz is teaching people about energy management, as well. We need to be taking regular breaks, eating healthfully, resting appropriately, and staying attuned to our peak work times so that we support ourselves in trying to focus.

**Overall, to Complete your actions you need a WHY, which is what we discussed in our Get Started chapter.** Knowing the deeper reasons for your work make the tasks evident and more internally motivated. The more clarity you have around your WHY, the more you will accomplish. If you didn't work through that, go back and do it now and write it down on your note-taking guide.

## *Correct*

I believe that any system is incomplete without a regular evaluation of how it's working—a feedback loop. I could have taught you 4 "C's" ending in Complete, and it still would have made sense, but making adjustments to your systems is as important as all of the other elements. That is why pencils have erasers!

**Take time out to review your systems, decide what's working and not working for you, and adjust to changing priorities.** Pay attention to new solutions and methods so that you can improve over time. Travel, job changes, and other life transitions can mean adjustments are needed.

"Correct" means that on a regular basis you are:

- ✓ **Paying attention to new methods of Capturing.** Is there some new software or a new product that would be helpful to your process?

- ✓ **Assessing whether your methods are working effectively.** Is anything falling through the cracks?

- ✓ **Asking yourself my favorite lazy-person questions:**

    - o   How can I do this better?

    - o   How can I do this faster?

    - o   How can I not do this at all?

- ✓ **Re-prioritizing your tasks and projects based on changes that have occurred**. This may mean ultimately deciding not to do some of the tasks you committed to doing before.

I firmly believe that choice management is very personal and unique, and people may need to change their systems periodically because they get bored or their circumstances are different. **One size does NOT fit all. Don't be afraid to Correct and try something new** until it works just right for your brain and your style! Need help? See our resources at the end of the book in our Get Help chapter.

## Calendar Strategies

Your calendar is a very special and sacred tool for managing your choices. **Do your best to have only one calendar for your life, rather than trying to split your work life and personal life into two systems.** Google Calendar actually does a fantastic job if you must separate these—you can keep a work calendar and personal calendar and merge them and separate them as needed for synchronizing and sharing and viewing. In general, however, having more than one calendar causes conflict and confusion when things are missed.

**Use your calendar for items that are specific to occur on a particular day and/or a particular time.** If you must do something on January 15, it needs to be on your calendar, either with or without a specific time. If you must do something sometime before January 15, you can put that on your task list noting the deadline. You could also schedule specific times to work on it leading up to the deadline, which is even better.

**When you make an appointment, try to capture everything you can onto the calendar so you can discard the related paper.** If it's a party invitation, you can note the address, driving directions, what to bring, what to wear, and other information and discard the invitation itself. Make a game of it! Try to get rid of as much paper as you can, and capture everything into your trusted tools. (Remember the Bookmark Principle!)

**When you add something to your calendar, ask yourself this question:**

---

**What could I do before, during, or after this appointment to improve it?**

---

Prepare for it, bring something to it, follow up after it… whatever that is, schedule it now or put it on your task list. Need to buy a gift, bring a dish, study something prior to the appointment? Need to bring a pen for taking notes, or business cards or brochures? Need to write a thank you note or send more information after the fact?

**This one question will improve your interactions, your efficiency, and your relationships!** Your meetings will be more productive, your last-minute rush errands will be minimized, and your friends and associates will appreciate your thoughtfulness and foresight.

## Smarter Scheduling

I made a video with several calendar tips and tricks, which you can see on your video tutorials page at *clutterdiet.com/homeofficevideos.*

**Making thorough notations on your calendar appointments can save you tons of time, money, and confusion.** Here are some ways to make consistent notes in your appointments-- things they don't teach you in school!

**The acronym TBD means "To Be Determined."** I use this when I want to hold a slot on my calendar but I don't know exactly what time I'm going to have the appointment yet or where I'm going to meet this person. I write "Time TBD," "Place TBD," or both "Time & Place TBD" on the appointment to remind myself that those decisions have not yet been made.

**Indicate your RSVP and registration information for parties and conferences so you'll know whether you've committed to attend.** Sometimes you put an event like a conference or a seminar on your calendar really far in advance because you want to have it on your radar, but you are not sure when the time gets closer if you have actually paid your registration fee or told the people you are coming. Write "RSVP-Yes" on the appointment or a note that says "registered 10/12/12—ticket on bulletin board."

**Establish who is calling whom for phone meetings.** When you have a phone appointment, sometimes you waste five or ten minutes crossing over each other, either both calling at the same time or waiting for the other person to call. Communicate about this deliberately as you set the appointment time, and find a consistent way to note this for yourself. For example, if someone else is calling me, I put her name first on the appointment: "Stacey calling." And if I'm calling her, I write, "Call Stacey."

**For in-person meetings, always exchange mobile numbers if possible.** People are often running five or ten minutes late, you might be running late, or there might be some kind of emergency and you need to reach them. Usually I put the person's mobile number right into my calendar appointment, even if I have the number in my contacts, because it's handier in a pinch.

**Always over-communicate time zone information when scheduling with non-local people.** When I have a phone call with someone in New York I always say, "2:00 PM Central, 3:00 PM Eastern." I say both times every time, and even when I do that, people still get confused. If you use Microsoft Outlook, Google Calendar, and other electronic calendars, you can indicate the time zone right in the appointment so you're not confused yourself, and it will always show up correctly even if you are traveling.

**If you need to share calendars with others for easier scheduling and reference**, I can heartily recommend both Google Calendar and Cozi. Cozi is made for families, with color-coding for each family member, and it synchronizes with Outlook and other calendars as well. For synchronizing Outlook with Google Calendar, try GSyncIt software.

## Birthdays

Calendars are not just for work-- they are also for fun! Remembering birthdays of friends and family is a way to show your love and friendship that takes very little effort. Here are several ways to manage birthdays effectively:

**Flag yourself on the first day of each month (or the first Tuesday, or whatever day makes sense for you) to check all birthdays for that month and get cards and gifts ready or scheduled to buy.** You can skim through your calendar to check for the month ahead, or you can start a "perpetual calendar" like the free spreadsheet we have for you at *www.clutterdiet.com/freetips* (on the left side of the page).

**Use SendOutCards.com where they have a reminder system for you, as well as the capability of setting up greeting cards to be sent as far in advance as you like.** These cards can be customized with your own photo or artwork, your own handwriting font, and your own scanned in signature. These cards save me a lot of time and help me stay in touch much more easily.

If you use Outlook, use this fantastic trick to plug birthdays into your calendar automatically: Open a contact and click Details, where a field for "Birthday" (and Anniversary) will appear. If you enter the person's birthdate in this field, Outlook will automatically populate the birthday into your calendar as a recurring annual event!

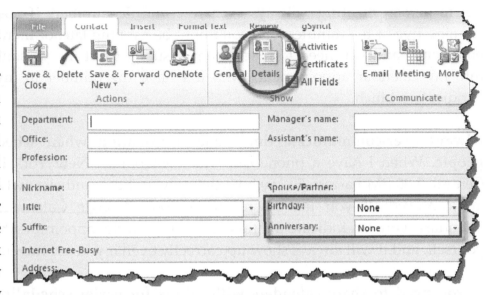

**Facebook will send you reminders once a week of your friends' birthdays.** You can check this weekly email and set up emails and task reminders for yourself to send the proper wishes at the right time.

## Task List

**Just as I advise you to have one calendar, I also advise you to have one master task list.**

**Accurately prioritizing what you need to do is literally impossible if you don't have everything in one place to gain visibility to it all.** How can you decide what to do right now if some things are written on a notepad in front of you, some are in your purse on the back of an envelope, and some are in an older list on your smartphone? Choose a primary tool and stick with it—be as consistent and disciplined as possible.

**I prefer electronic task lists, because they allow you to categorize, sort, filter, and prioritize your master list based on your needs at the moment.** I encourage people to use Microsoft Outlook, particularly if they already use it for email. As you'll note in our Email chapter, you can click and drag emails to Tasks, where the information from the email becomes either attached to the task or pasted into the Notes field for future reference.

**I also prefer using Outlook because my tasks have Cues built in.** You can Cue a task for any date and exact time, and you can snooze the reminders for a day or a week or even five minutes. I can alert myself of something and take one action step, then Cue it for the next appropriate time.

**If you want to keep things simple, you can make one notebook your master task list, and write everything on it linearly and keep going, making new pages, crossing off as you go.** That method is the simplest way to do it, but you still may want to recopy your list and refine it by hand at some points.

**If you use an electronic option, make sure it's with you on your smartphone.** Your list is your guiding force for the Committed items you want to do in your work and life, and you need to be able to access it at any time!

**Some people like to start each day by looking at their master list and making a daily list for that day, maybe on a sticky note or sheet of paper.** I agree that is very satisfying and provides focus, especially if you only choose 3-5 things you're going to get done before anything else. If you need more to do, go back to the master list.

## How to Sort Your Tasks

The most confusing thing for people is usually how to sort and prioritize tasks in a list. Since I believe that this is part of your unique fingerprint of what works for you and your situation, this answer will vary greatly.

**Many people find categorizing things by** *when they need to be done* **is the most effective.** You can categorize each item as "Today," "This Week," "This Month," "This Year," and "Future." Personally, I find this method gives me the most peace of mind. Each time I review my calendar and task list, I reposition some of these as things change. You can also use 1-2-3, Low-Normal-High or A-B-C prioritization for the same kind of effect.

**Others think you should categorize tasks by context and action.** Calls, Errands, Actions, Discussions... these are also quite effective. When you sit down to make calls, you know all the calls you need to make are right there. When you are going to run errands, all of the errands are grouped together for efficiency. But do they all need to be done at that same time? Maybe not.

If you're using Outlook, Toodledo, RememberTheMilk, or other fairly high-powered lists, you can sort by context and action as Categories, and use the Low-Normal-High priority indicator to choose when they get done, as a combination you can sort as needed.

**Consider these choices and group things as they make best sense for you and your situation.** There is no wrong answer if it works for you!

**But keep it simple. One of the pitfalls I definitely see is that people try to overcomplicate and engineer their lists as a way to avoid work.** Anyone relate? ;)

**Whatever your style of sorting, make sure you have a Future category to capture ideas for low-priority tasks you may want to do down the road.** You can put these ideas in Evernote and tag them "Future," if you like, or make a category of Tasks in Outlook for this, or start a special page in your notebook. I have some Future tasks noted like "Buy tickets to see Brian Setzer in concert" and "Create a book club guide for my book."

**Wording of your tasks is important! Use a strong verb for the first word, like Call, Write, Research, Read, Watch, or Buy.** Think about the next action that is truly required to make progress, and use THAT verb to begin the phrase.

## Projects

It's worth noting here that there is a difference between projects and tasks.

**Projects are a collection of tasks that combine together to accomplish a goal. They have a beginning and end.**

For example, a project might be "Plan a party." The tasks are: Set date and time, write guest list, create invitations, mail invitations, create menu, buy food, etc.

Each task needs to get done at the right time, and you can plug those into your calendar and task list separately to make sure they happen.

Each project can have a planning page where you strategize your tasks, or a separate task category can be called "Projects" in Outlook where each task lists your planning information for that project. Here's what that might look like in Outlook.

I like Avery 72257 Extended Edge Document Sleeves for my projects, which are re-usable plastic folders. I put labels on them from my label maker, and when the project concludes, I peel off the label easily and use the folder again. I like them because they are very sturdy, come in different colors, have a see-through front and are closed on two sides, so that the papers don't fall out easily. Each one of my trips out I consider a project of its own, so every trip has a travel folder made from one of these Avery sleeves.

More about Projects in our next chapter... as we learn about how to process our information.

# PROCESSING INFORMATION

**Remember that childhood game, Rock-Paper-Scissors?**

If you're not familiar with it, two people each choose to show a hand signal on a count of three, and the winner is determined by which hand signal trumps the other:

- Rock crushes Scissors
- Scissors cut Paper
- Paper covers Rock

It's fun, but **it's really a decision-making tool disguised as a game. That's why we're going to take the fun spirit of it and use it for decision-making about our information.**

**All information can be classified and sorted as Action, Reference, or Trash.** You can remember this because it spells the word ART, and you can also remember it because it corresponds to our rock-paper-scissors hand signals.

## ACTION (To Do)

Paper symbolizes information in front of us ready for work.

## REFERENCE (To Keep)

Rock symbolizes a paperweight holding down information we want to keep, or a fist holding onto something.

# TRASH (Recycle, Shred)

Scissors symbolize cutting and shredding the information.

**So let's take an imaginary example paper inbox and sort it out with this model.**

There is a flowchart here in the book to follow along, but it may be easier for you to view and follow if you print it out from the web as a separate PDF at *clutterdiet.com/officeflowchart*.

You have Captured information-- in this case it's paper-- captured into your physical inbox on your desk.

**The first thing you want to do is pull the reading material out.** Magazines, journals, and catalogs are thick and bulky, and they belong in your reading basket elsewhere. Taking this information out first makes the rest of the pile much less intimidating.

**Open up envelopes with a letter opener,** which is a very handy tool to keep in your inbox. **Now discard the envelopes...** I have seen clients who have a habit of re-folding everything and putting it back into the envelopes, which doubles your work later.

**The next step is to do what I call "Scanalyzing."** From years of working with clients, I have noticed **there is a skill of skimming information quickly to understand 1) what it is and 2) what it "wants" from you.** Rarely is there a need to read every word of a document when you are sorting. You can read the first and last sentences or paragraphs, along with anything that is bolded or highlighted, and look for phrases like "Please do (x) by January 15," or "Will you let us know (x)?" You are looking for what actions are required, if any, from this document.

As you Scanalyze, you will then be asking the most pivotal question of all:

## ACTION, REFERENCE, or TRASH?

The answer to that question will lead you to the next step. Let's say the letter you are looking at is one that requires action, for example, an invitation to a dinner party from a vendor.

Now you are looking at whether to Commit to this action, and how.

**Ask "What is the next step?"**

The next step for this dinner party invitation is to check your calendar to see your availability. You are available, and you know that attending this dinner and developing this relationship with your vendor is aligned with your goals.

You'll then ask, do I want to:

---

### Handle It Now,
### Handle It Later, or
### Hand It Off?

---

**In this case, you will Handle It Now.** Many of my colleagues suggest a "two-minute rule," and I agree. If you can handle it in less than two minutes, you probably should go ahead and do it. So you will go to your preferred calendar tool to Commit to the appointment, and you'll want to Cue yourself for any appropriate next actions.

When you put something on your calendar, as I said in the previous chapter, it's a good idea to ask yourself, **"What could I do before, during, or after this appointment to improve it?"** If there are any further actions that would be smart, such as replying to RSVP, buying a bottle of wine to take to the dinner, and writing a thank-you note after it's over, put those in your calendar and/or task list as needed with proper Cues.

Now when those actions are Cued, Complete them and follow your plan, Correcting your systems as you review each week.

You want to process each item in your inbox (physical or electronic) this same way.

**FOR JUNK MAIL:**

Check out an app for iPhone and Android called Paper Karma. Register for free, snap a photo of the mailing label with your phone's camera, and you're done! They will unsubscribe you.

Also check out CatalogChoice.org to manage subscriptions to catalogs.

For other Action items in your inbox, you may decide to **Handle It Later**. You will want to have some Quick Action trays or baskets set up for common actions in your particular situation. The A-R-T Chart on the next page will help you understand where to put everything. Go to *clutterdiet.com/artchart* to save and print this chart as its own separate PDF.

# The A-R-T Chart

| 3 Kinds of Info | Types | What Does That Mean? | Examples | Where Do I Keep It? |
|---|---|---|---|---|
| **A** "Action" To Do | **Quick Actions** | Information representing simple things you need to do. | • Bills<br>• Forms<br>• Greeting cards<br>• Addresses to enter<br>• Receipts for a return<br>• Something simple you're waiting on | Stacking trays work for most people; possibly small "piles" if that is your style; baskets; vertical sorters; or folders. Emails may be kept until acted upon or made into tasks. |
| | **Projects** | Information you are gathering up in one place to do a larger, longer-term action, with a beginning and end to them. | • Planning a party<br>• Kids' activities<br>• Remodeling projects<br>• Business projects<br>• Current year's income tax file<br>• Travel folders | Usually a combination of hanging folders and manila folders in a drawer work best, sometimes bins if the project is very large or bulky. Also try folders in a wire desktop sorter. Electronic folders for email or documents, or Outlook tasks. |
| **R** "Reference" To Keep | **Fingertips** | Info you need to refer to quickly and often. | • Frequently called numbers list<br>• School schedules<br>• Lunch menus<br>• Chores lists<br>• "Cheat Sheets" | Bulletin board, under glass on your desk, in your Family Binder, Evernote, smartphone apps. |
| | **Handy** | Recent, relevant info you just need or want to save for later. Nothing you need to do. | • Insurance paperwork<br>• Home maintenance and warranty info<br>• Medical information<br>• Articles | Filing cabinets, "To Be Filed" basket. You can file alphabetically, numerically, or use categories and color-coding. Electronic folders or Evernote. |

| | | | | |
|---|---|---|---|---|
| | **Arms' Length** | Archives- an older version of Handy Reference that you want to move out of your way. | • Older tax records<br>• Real estate documents<br>• Older investment info | "Bankers Boxes" or plastic file box containers, DVDs, external hard drives |
| **"Trash"**<br><br>Delete, shred or recycle | **Trash or Recycling** | Please do recycle if you possibly can! | • Junk mail<br>• Older catalogs and magazines | You may want a personal recycling bin near your own work area. Make sure your trash can is large enough to hold 2-3 days of trash! Petite, decorative bathroom cans need not apply! |
| | **Shredding** | Make sure you are careful to shred things that have account numbers or personal information. | • Credit card offers<br>• Password information<br>• Old financial records | You may want a personal shredding box near your own work area if you have to take things elsewhere to shred. |

Our flowchart on the next page will walk you through all of the steps, and you can save and print that as its own separate PDF at *clutterdiet.com/officeflowchart*.

Our next chapter is Paper Reference, where we'll get into what to do with the things you want to keep.

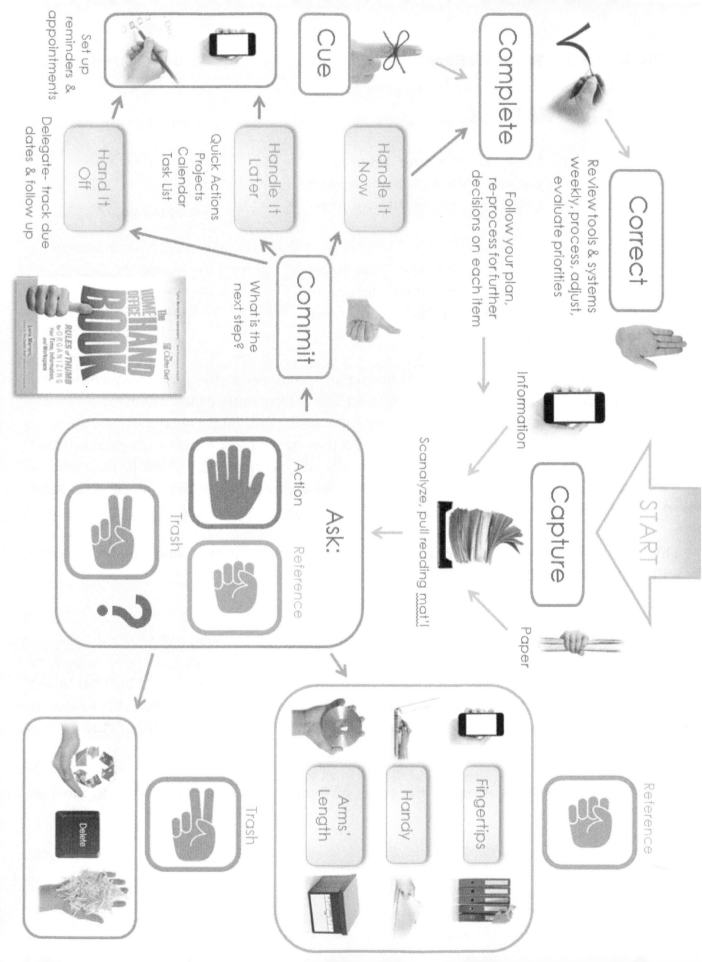

START

Capture

Paper

Scanalyze, pull reading mat'l

Information

Ask:
Action
Reference
Trash

Reference

Arms' Length
Handy
Fingertips

Trash

Delete

Commit
What is the next step?

Handle It Now

Handle It Later
Quick Actions
Projects
Calendar
Task List

Hand It Off
Delegate- track due dates & follow up

Set up reminders & appointments

Cue

Complete
Follow your plan, re-process for further decisions on each item

Correct
Review tools & systems weekly, process, adjust, evaluate priorities

The HOME OFFICE HAND BOOK
RULES of THUMB for ORGANIZING Your Time, Information, and Workspace
Lorie Marrero

from **The Home Office Handbook** by Lorie Marrero

www.clutterdiet.com/homeoffice

# PAPER REFERENCE

**So you want to keep it for future reference… before you do, are you sure?** Many of my colleagues agree with me that 80% of what we file we never look at again!

As we mentioned before in the Processing Information chapter, **there are three levels of reference information, based on how readily you need to put your hands on it:**

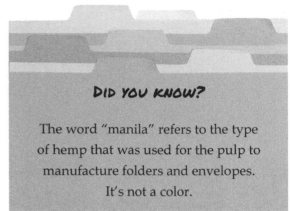

**DID YOU KNOW?**

The word "manila" refers to the type of hemp that was used for the pulp to manufacture folders and envelopes. It's not a color.

- ☑ **Fingertips:** Quick reference information you need to grab frequently and immediately, such as "cheat sheets" and lists of frequently called numbers.
- ☑ **Handy:** Recent and relevant reference information you might need to consult.
- ☑ **Arms' Length:** Older archived files you may never need to consult again, but you need to keep them just in case. Tax records and old client files might be examples of Arms' Length information. You want these archives out of the way of your daily workspace.

**This chapter will cover the PAPER form of Reference information, and the next chapter will deal with the ELECTRONIC INFORMATION.**

## *Fingertips Reference*

Your "cheat sheets," charts, phone lists, and other grab-and-go information need to be very close to your workspace, usually in a strategically located binder or on a bulletin board near your desk. This information is what you need immediately when that client calls, or when you're doing routine tasks, or you otherwise need to refer to something quickly and move forward.

For a business, here are some of the types of information you might want to have in Fingertips format:

- ✓ Daily checklists
- ✓ Frequently used procedures
- ✓ Frequently called numbers
- ✓ Phone system instructions
- ✓ Graphic design style guides (colors, fonts)
- ✓ HTML code cheat sheets
- ✓ Vendor lists and ordering info
- ✓ Formulas (I once organized a chemistry lab!)
- ✓ Shipping box sizes and pricing
- ✓ Chart of Accounts for bookkeeping
- ✓ Customer service policies
- ✓ Passwords (but do this securely! See our section on passwords in the Electronic Information chapter for help with this)
- ✓ Annual calendars for bookkeeping or holidays

Binders are ideal for this information, and using plastic page protectors is also a good idea. Empty page protectors can be already put into the binder waiting for new items, and they allow you to add something quickly without punching holes in the paper. Of course, they also help protect the paper long-term from fingerprints, dirt and spills.

A "Family Binder" is something we describe in more detail in our Family & Home chapter, and it is definitely a Fingertips reference. There you can read about how to set one up for school, medical, child care, neighborhood, sports and activities, and other family information.

A bulletin board is also helpful for Fingertips information, but make sure that you don't clutter your bulletin board with too many other items that might have a better home elsewhere.

See our Electronic Information chapter for ways to keep your Fingertips information electronically.

# Handy Reference: Creating and Maintaining Files

An entirely paperless office is highly unlikely, at least for the foreseeable future. Human beings still like to have some things printed out and in their hands to read and keep. As accessible and easy as our smartphones are to use, sometimes it's still faster and easier to jot something down on a piece of paper.

Until something drastically changes, we are still going to have some paper in our offices, but we'll probably continue to have less of it. These next sections will help you deal with the paper you want to keep handy "just in case."

## Love Your Filing Cabinet

Doing your filing is admittedly not a jolly good time, so at least make sure you're not making it worse by having creaky, rusty old filing cabinets with drawers that stick!

Investing in good quality filing cabinets does *not* mean spending a lot of money. If your city has a used office furniture liquidator, you can get killer deals on scratch-and-dent filing cabinets there (along with shelving, desks, and even sticky notes and markers sometimes!). You can also check thrift stores like Goodwill®. Search Google for "used office furniture" along with the name of your city to find these resources.

**Consider lateral files instead of traditional drawers that run front to back**, because they give greater visibility to the entire row of folders at once, and you can easily reach any file instead of having to dig and tug at the ones in the back. If you have a lateral cabinet, you'll get some extra space for storage alongside the rows of letter-sized folders, where you can store things like boxes of checks, landscaping plans, blueprints, and other oversized or bulky documents.

**Test all drawers before buying to make sure they work smoothly.** Check to see if the keys are present that fit the locks, and make sure there are hanging folder rails included. Don't under-buy! Buy cabinets that are sturdy and will meet your needs for years to come.

**When using your filing cabinets, don't stuff your file drawers too full.** Are you avoiding filing because you can't stand plunging your hand into the tight drawer, getting paper cuts, and fighting to get the papers into the folders? Adjust your drawer space so that you can easily get the folders in and out and leave some room to grow, too. If you are running out of space, guess what? It's time to shred, recycle, and archive older files to another location to free up some space.

If possible, **take the time to label the outside of each drawer with a range of alphabetical indications or numbers,** saving you a little frustration and time from opening the wrong drawers as you file and retrieve.

Most quality filing cabinets come with this capability, **but if you don't have hanging folder rails, purchase inexpensive ones at any office supply store,** assemble them, and drop them into the drawers.

## Folders: Don't Settle For Just Plain Manila

Manila folders are the traditional basic unit of filing, but they are not the only option.

**I generally recommend that people use hanging file folders**, the type that most people refer to by the brand "Pendaflex®" (The Pendaflex company makes many other products, but I have found people use that word just like the word "Kleenex" is referred to tissues.)

**Hanging folders keep your files from falling all over each other and slumping down in the drawer.** As I always say, the goal of every organizing project is visibility, and you want to enable all folders to be visible and avoid the smaller ones sliding down and disappearing.

Hanging folders are not a must, but **if you don't use them, at least make sure that your file drawer has a sliding rear support that pushes the folders up into the front of the drawer** to avoid the slumping problem.

**When you use hanging folders, you do NOT have to put another manila-style folder inside of it!** People have told me they think it's double the work to use hanging folders because they thought they had to make two folders and two labels for every file. NOPE! If the material is not going to be referenced often, just make the hanging folder and plop in the papers and you're done.

**If you anticipate needing to access the papers more often, or if you need to create subdivisions within the file, you can add an interior folder to create these sections and to make it easier to remove and transport the papers.** You can use traditional manila ones, or just go crazy and get leopard print folders if you like. Whatever makes you smile! Filing's not super fun, so make it easier any way you can.

**I recommend buying high-quality, brand-name hanging folders,** since the cheaper ones will fall apart over time. The glue will loosen on the metal rails and they will slide out.

## Rules of Thumb for Labeling Folders

Feel like you missed that day in school when they taught you how to put the little plastic tabs on the file folders? Well, don't worry, nobody ever teaches us this stuff... you didn't miss it. I have always felt like this was missing from our education system. Most of us learn filing and other organizational habits by observing what our parents did, or our first boss... or by observing what they *didn't* do.

As for rules, these filing rules are the ones I follow and teach my clients, but if you have an existing habit or strong preference for another way, by all means, do that. **What's important is to be consistent within your own system.**

**To handwrite, or machine label?** Personal preference wins on this question. Handwritten labels are much faster to make, and if your priority is speed over beauty, that's perfectly fine. I do suggest always using a marker that makes dark, visible lines and using the same consistent pen if possible. You can tie a string (or glue a magnet) to your favorite folder-labeling pen and attach it to the inside of your file drawer so it's always there.

**My preference is to print labels,** either with a handheld label maker or a printer. Just know that if you choose printing, you are adding another step to making each new file. Personally, I prefer the legibility of a printed label over my handwriting which varies quite a bit, so I make the effort, and my clients also usually prefer labels. **My logic: If it's truly valuable enough to actually keep the paper instead of scanning it, it's worthy of having its own printed label.**

**Avery 11136 Worksaver Tab Inserts for Hanging File Folders can be typed up onscreen in a batch and printed with any office laser or inkjet printer.** These printable sheets are a staple item when I create a filing system, but they are not usually kept in stock in office supply stores, so I order them online (they cost about $2.00 per pack).

**Tabs on the front or back?** I like to place my tabs on the front of the folder, because when I pull them that motion opens up the folder. Again, this is a personal preference, so start somewhere and be consistent.

**How do you stagger the tabs across the folders?** You don't have to utilize every slot provided. I use only two positions for the tabs, and that positioning creates two solid rows of alternating tabs so that your eye can follow the labels more easily in the drawer. Doing it this way also eliminates that decision or that uncertainty about where to stagger that tab across on the slots.

**Open your file drawer and note whether left or right positioning is best.** If you're sitting in your chair facing a lateral drawer on its right side like I am in the photo above, you'll want to place your tabs on the left side of the folders. This picture shows exactly what I am talking about by alternating two positions. See how neat that looks? So much easier to read, and if you have to add new folders between them, they will never be so far out of alignment as to merit re-doing the whole row. Don't worry about it!

Later we'll talk about numerical search filing, and if you number your files, those two rows end up neatly being even and odd numbers. Very cool.

**What about thick files? Many people don't know about "box-bottom" folders.** These folders are sold in assorted widths, but I usually buy the 2" size. The bottom is creased and shaped to reinforce holding a large amount of paper. Think twice before filing documents like these, however, as they may be better held in a binder on a shelf... and could you keep it electronically instead?

## Thumbs Down to...

**...Color-coding.** Thumbs down? What? That's probably not what you were expecting me to say.

Color-coding of files can be very effective if used in a limited way. But more often, people create elaborate systems with their colors that make it ultimately much harder to maintain their files.

- Too many colors gives you yet another decision to make about your papers
- Too many colors are hard to remember and keep track of (Was green for personal, or financial?)
- Hard to stock all the colors, and if you run out, you can't file
- Hard for other people to follow if they are helping to file or needing to retrieve

If you must color-code, keep it simple and use it to differentiate entire sets of files (like client files vs. financial) or just have 2-3 colors that are very easy to remember.

**...Legal-sized folders.** Bigger is not necessarily better! Legal-sized cabinets are harder to find, the folders cost more, and they are rarely needed unless you have a profession that regularly uses that paper size.

**...Paper clips.** Paper clips do have their uses, but I do not recommend that they are used inside reference files long-term. They grab onto other papers, fall off, and cause all kinds of mischief. I think staples are better.

## "To Be Filed," or NOT "To Be Filed"?

We've described in our chapter about processing that you can set up a basket or tray of things "To Be Filed." You can choose what works best for you—filing things in the moment as they come (continuous processing) vs. filing the whole basket at one time (batch processing). Each way has advantages, since filing in the moment means it's not procrastinated, and filing in a batch provides some efficiency with the tools and supplies, and you'll run into older papers and decide not to keep them after all. See which method you prefer. If you want to encourage yourself to file in the moment as you go or at the end of each day, dispense with having a "To Be Filed" basket as you will certainly use it.

If someone else is going to do your filing, you will need a place to put those papers until your helper can get to them. LUCKY YOU and great job for delegating! When you place papers into your "To Be Filed" basket, write keywords and instructions either directly on it or using a sticky note so this person will not have to read your mind. Providing good instructions means your filing system will be better built on the way you personally think.

## The Traditional Way to File: Alphabetically

Everyone is familiar with the traditional way to file, by naming folders and filing them in order from A-Z.

If your filing needs are relatively simple, alphabetical filing is a terrific solution. Pick up a bank statement and file it under "Bank Statements 2012." Got a client named John Smith? File it under S for "Smith, John," and you're done!

Here are some strategies to make your alphabetical filing system work better long term.

- **Create a filing index.** When you have finished setting up your initial system, take a moment to make a list in a spreadsheet or word processing document of all of the folders in order, so you can quickly gain visibility to the choices in your file drawer without opening it. An index is particularly useful if you are delegating filing, because you can refer to it before writing instructions on the pages.

- **Be consistent.** If you see a pattern, take the time to match it with future folders. For example, if you label something "Medical- Judy" and another folder needs to be made for a family member named George, a good approach is to name his folder "Medical- George," and end up with all of the medical folders next to each other in the drawer.
- **Review your folders and clean them up regularly.** Once or twice a year, you can quickly scan through all of the folder names and see if there are duplicates or any patterns that need adjusting. Make a new file index as often as needed to keep it fresh and current and useful.

## The Alternative: Numerical Search Filing

As you will see, I am a huge fan of Numerical Search Filing.

I am so happy to provide a training video just for you, the purchasers of this book, on exactly how to do this! You can view it on your video tutorials page at *clutterdiet.com/homeofficevideos*.

**Alphabetical filing has a serious limitation… you can file something only one way.** With something like a car insurance paper, you will likely have a hard time deciding what to name it. Here are some of your choices, **which one do you think is correct?**

- State Farm
- Insurance
- Auto Insurance
- Car Insurance
- Honda
- Vehicles

Trick question! All of these are technically "correct." **But how will you remember later what you chose?**

We're all accustomed to being able to find almost anything with Google, so **why not be able to "Google" your own file drawer?**

Numerical filing allows you to do just that. Imagine that you no longer have to decide what to name a folder... you just name it all of the possibilities at once.

Here's how it works:

- ✓ **Set up some hanging file folders with numbered labels, such as "Reference 1," "Reference 2," "Reference 3," "Reference 4," and so on.** I recommend starting with 50-100 folders since they are easy to make and set up quickly. Once you set up these folders, which are ready in advance of any filing you need to do, you are DONE making folders until they are all full.
- ✓ **Use one of the tools given below to set up an easy searchable database of your files.** Basically, each folder in your drawer will be represented by:
    - o A Number, ("Reference 1," 2, etc.)
    - o A primary File Name ("Car Insurance"- pick something and go with it)
    - o A Keyword field to describe it (a place to put all of the searchable terms you might think of later).
- ✓ **Grab a stack of some papers and plow through them at your desk before you ever reach for the file cabinet.** Take the first paper, type in a primary File Name, add some Keywords, and write the number of that file at the top of the paper.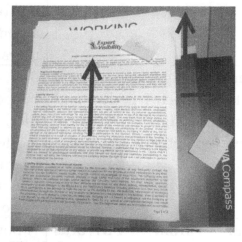
- ✓ **Make a new staggered pile of the papers you've entered into the system, readying them to be placed in the folders.** When you're finished entering the information into the database, pick up the papers and quickly drop them into their corresponding numbered folders. That's it.
- ✓ **When it's time to retrieve, open your database and search.** The results will show you which numbered folder to retrieve your papers from, and it takes only seconds. Time it!
- ✓ **Make adjustments like adding new keywords and consolidating files as you go.** You will discover that your numerical filing system actually improves over time, as your keywording makes your search results richer and more helpful. Natural cross-referencing occurs as you see your search results and realize you have more information about that topic than you originally remembered.

Here are some options for creating your Numerical Search filing system:

| Option | Pros | Cons |
|---|---|---|
| **Excel Spreadsheet** (I have a free one already set up at *clutterdiet.com/freetips* that you can download. Find it on the left side of the page.) | FREE, most people already know how to use it, great for simple home filing systems. Can use Google Docs to put info in the cloud (but my spreadsheet will lose some features). | Clumsy for searching and file row numbers can be confusing being listed next to your file folder numbers. Not good for larger filing systems or for multiple users. |
| **Evernote** (use a separate Evernote Notebook for your filing system, one note per file) | FREE, easy to use, flexible, located in cloud, as a mobile app, and on desktop. Can also add photos and attachments to a note to put in other digital info to accompany the file. Multiple users can share the data. | Slightly clumsy as it is not originally built for this purpose, but better than Excel option. Need to keyword open numerical files with "#empty" so you can see what folders are open and available for new files. |
| **ThePaperTiger.com** (cloud option, which I prefer) and **Paper Tiger** software (desktop option) | Built exactly for this purpose, easy merging of files, lots of great features, located in the cloud, multiple user options, multiple sets of files can be handled in the same database. | Annual or monthly fees, but they are very reasonable. Desktop software option will need upgrades over time. May require training. |
| **iPEP from PBWorks** (created by my colleague and friend Barbara Hemphill) | A powerful cloud based collaboration tool & document mgmt system, customized to index physical files, in addition to electronic. Multi-user options available, enterprise level security. | Generally better for businesses than for home use, reasonable cost involved, may require training. |

## General Filing Rules of Thumb

Regardless of the methodology used to file, there are some consistent practices that will help keep things in order.

- **New in front, or new in back?** If papers need to be in sequential order, such as dated account statements, be consistent about whether the newer papers go in front or in back of the file. I prefer back, since when stacked on a table, the papers go from oldest to newest, top to bottom.

- **File in groups of years, such as "Bank Statements 2012," Bank Statements 2011" so that it's easier to purge and archive later.** If you wish to file general account information like terms and conditions with these statements, separate the "evergreen" papers from the dated statements with an interior folder.

- **Keep it simple.** With the exceptions of business vs. personal sets of files and sets of alphabetical files for clients or customers, **reference filing typically works best long term with ONE continuous system** instead of subdividing it with different drawers, locations, colors, or sections.

- **For help naming your files, consult our Common Household File Headings chart on the next few pages.** We usually separate car insurance files from car maintenance files, but if you want to put it all together and call it "Car Stuff," that's okay. The key is that the names be **Meaningful** and **Memorable** so that you'll remember them when it's time to file again.

- **For your monthly paid bills, receipts and statements, dispense with trying to file these alphabetically by vendor or account and try using a brown, January-December accordion file for each year's papers.** I like the kind that are open-top (no flap closure) and already labeled with the months. Each month after you pay your bills and receive your regular account statements, file them quickly together in that month's section and be done with it. This system works for the majority of people and simplifies things greatly. If you need to find something, you can locate the transaction within QuickBooks or your online banking data, referring you to the date and thus the correct compartment.

## Thoughts on Scanning

**A modern home office probably does need a scanner, but the type certainly depends upon your needs.** If you scan large quantities of paper frequently, you'll need to buy a solid and reliable piece of equipment that processes stacks efficiently, and possibly you'll want to consider a local scanning service to outsource the work regularly.

There may be a new pile of "To Be Scanned" items that gets created. **Know that this bottleneck may occur and have a plan to regularly scan things,** just as you would have a plan to regularly file. This job is yet another good one for your friendly neighborhood teenager!

Even the IRS accepts some scanned documents nowadays, but do take care to still retain some formal documents in their original paper form, such as important contracts, identification like marriage licenses and birth certificates, and other hard-to-replace items.

**Here are some questions to consider for purchasing a scanner or using a scanning service:**

- ☑ How fast does the scanner process a stack of paper?
- ☑ Does the scanner have an automatic document feeder, so that you don't have to "babysit" feeding a stack of paper through the machine?
- ☑ Does the scanner or scanning service process both fronts & backs of your pages?
- ☑ How do the resulting electronic documents get named and located on your hard drive? How does search and retrieval work?
- ☑ What format are the documents in when finished? PDF or a proprietary format? Be careful about proprietary formats, since your documents need to be readable far into the future and products, software, and companies can disappear over time.
- ☑ Is the output in color, black & white, or grayscale? Text-searchable "OCR" (Optical Character Recognition) scanning; or just graphic images of the page? What about highlighter marker usage on the pages—how does that effect the scanning? What about charts or photos that are scanned black & white- are they going to be readable?

## Common File Headings

Go to *clutterdiet.com/fileheadings* for a printable reference PDF of this chart.

| File Content Category | Suggested Titles | Comments |
| --- | --- | --- |
| Bank Statements | "(bank name) Checking (year)" or<br><br>"(bank name) Savings (year)" | Preferably filed with paid bills in a Jan-Dec accordion file. Strongly consider getting these statements electronically from their website and requesting paperless communication! If you do want these in with your main files, naming the folders by year and separating them out this way makes it easier to archive later. |
| Brokerage Statements | "Brokerage Statements 2005," 2006, 2007, etc., or investment company such as "Schwab (year)" or "Merrill Lynch (year)" | Strongly consider getting these statements electronically from their website and requesting paperless communication! Naming the folders by year and separating them out this way makes it easier to archive later. |
| Cars/Vehicles | "Chrysler Pacifica" (your car's make/model) | Contains all papers about initial purchase, registration, inspections, repairs, and other things unique to that vehicle. Separate the insurance and loan information into other folders (see Insurance, Loans). Keep the title in your Fire Safe (see Fire Safe). |
| Cards & Keepsakes | "Keepsakes-(name of person)" or "Memorabilia- | One folder for each family member- may need a bin rather than a folder if you like |

| File Content Category | Suggested Titles | Comments |
|---|---|---|
| | "(name of person)" | keeping a lot. See Family & Home chapter. |
| Career Planning | "Career Planning-(name of person)" | Resumes, performance reviews, goals, educational transcripts. |
| Child Care Information | "(name of child care provider/center)" or "Child Care" or "Babysitter Info" | Can also keep this in your Family Binder. Includes general information about day care policies and procedures and correspondence, or a list of babysitters' numbers and identification information. |
| Churches/Places of Worship, Clubs | "(name of organization)" | Contains general reference information about policies and other membership data. |
| Credit Card Information | "Bank of America Credit Card Account Info" (for specific account) or more generally, "Credit Card Info" | Recommended to save terms & conditions agreements and correspondence about the account itself (not the statements) in this file (the "evergreen" info). Usually okay to put different accounts' information together in one file since there may not be much for each. |
| Credit Card Statements | Recommended to file with paid bills in accordion file, but if not, title "MBNA Credit Card (year)" (your bank name + year) | File in Jan-Dec accordion file with paid bills instead of in the main files. Strongly consider getting these statements electronically from their website and requesting paperless communication! If you do file in your main files, naming the |

| File Content Category | Suggested Titles | Comments |
|---|---|---|
| | | folders by year and separating them out this way makes it easier to archive later. |
| Credit Reports | "Credit Reports" | We remind our paid Clutter Diet members to run these reports 3x a year. It's generally okay to shred the oldest one when you put a new one in the file. Keep the last year's reports for reference, unless there is a problem on one of them, in which case you will want to keep it until the problem is resolved. |
| Death or Family Information | "(name of loved one who has passed)" or "(Family Last Name) Information" or "(Name) Estate" | If you have planned a funeral or been involved in the loss of a loved one, you may have information that is important to keep. Death certificates are better kept under "Identification" or in a Fire Safe. |
| Decorating Ideas | "House Ideas," "Decorating Ideas" or other as you prefer | Contains clippings of things you like for your house, such as furniture or paint ideas. If you have a lot of these, you may want to make an accordion folder just for this that is separated with divisions by room. Could be a project file if you are actively redecorating. Also consider doing this on Pinterest instead of using paper. |
| Financial Planning | "Financial Planning," "Retirement Planning" | Contains general information about planning your investments, notes on any advice you've received, Social Security |

| File Content Category | Suggested Titles | Comments |
|---|---|---|
| | | statements, or articles related to this subject. |
| Fire Safe or Safe Deposit Box | (not a folder) | Having a fire safe or safe deposit box is a good idea for original documents that are difficult to replace, such as birth certificates, original deeds, and vehicle titles. Home inventory records are important too. Make copies of these documents to put into your Identification file for quicker access to the information. Can also use a product like the Vital Records PortaVault®. |
| Gift Certificates & Gift Cards | Gift Certificates | Create a file for temporary storage of gift certificates you haven't used. Set up a reminder as some will expire. |
| Gifts, Gift Ideas | "Gift Ideas" or "Gifts" | Ideas, lists and clippings from catalogs related to gifts you have given or might like to give. You can also use Evernote for this or a secret board on Pinterest. See your exclusive Evernote training at *clutterdiet.com/homeofficevideos*. |
| Health & Nutrition | "Health & Fitness" or "Nutrition" or "Wellness" | A common interest category, containing articles of interest about health and exercise and nutrition. |

| File Content Category | Suggested Titles | Comments |
|---|---|---|
| Holidays | "Christmas" or "Hanukkah" or other major holidays for your family | Contains information about previous years' completed plans for future reference. Active plans for this year can be a Project folder and relevant information can move here when finished. |
| Home Improvements & Repairs | "Home Improvements" or "(street name of your house) Home Improvements" | Keep receipts here for major home improvements and repairs, along with general information about your home's maintenance. No need to keep minor receipts such as exterminator services or carpet cleaning, unless there are termites involved or other issues beyond routine matters. |
| Humor | "Funny File," "Humor" | Your "Funny File" contains funny comic strip clippings, printouts of jokes, and other fun things people have shared with you. |
| Identification & Legal Papers | "Identification" | Voter registration cards, copies of birth certificates, marriage certificates and passports (keep originals in a fire safe if possible- see Fire Safe). |
| Income Tax | "Income Tax (year)" or "Taxes (year)" | One for each year, make some in advance. Put all papers in that were directly used to prepare the return, such as W-2s and 1099 year-end statements, any IRS correspondence, and also a copy of the |

| File Content Category | Suggested Titles | Comments |
|---|---|---|
| | | return itself. |
| Inspirations & Quotes | "Inspirations & Quotes," "Inspirations," "Spiritual" | You may like collecting favorite quotations or clippings of articles and stories that you relate to on a personal or spiritual level. |
| Insurance | Keep separate files for "Insurance-Auto," "Insurance-Property," "Insurance-Medical," "Insurance-Life," and "Insurance-Other" | Keep your policies and most recent correspondence here for each category. Ask for paperless options! For medical, you may need to have Project files that are for active papers, such as "Medical Claims to Be Filed" and "Medical Claims Pending." This folder is for general information and completed issues. |
| Inventory | "Home Inventory" or "Inventory" | If you have taken a home inventory, keep the most current list here, and a copy in your fire safe or safe deposit box. |
| Investment Information | "Stocks," "Investments," or "(name of particular stock, bond, or fund)" | For general information and correspondence about your investments. You might want to split this into various folders if you have a lot of them. This is not for the statements; those need to be done separately (see Brokerage Statements). |
| Loans | "Bank of America Car Loan," "Chevrolet Loan" | Contains all loan papers and correspondence for that account. Consider |

| File Content Category | Suggested Titles | Comments |
|---|---|---|
| | (your information as you will remember it) | requesting paperless statements, or filing statements in Jan-Dec accordion file with bills. |
| Maps & Directions | "Maps & Directions" | Contains driving directions and maps for things you will likely visit again. If you just have a few, you can file under "Travel- Places We've Been." Consider using Evernote for this, and also consider that most maps are obsolete the moment they are printed and typically you'll use an online map or GPS. |
| Medical | "Medical-(name of person)" | Medical history, important test results, medical records, vaccinations/shot records for each person in the family. |
| Mortgage | "(street name of your house) Mortgage" | Contains correspondence and other general information about your home loan. Consider getting a paperless statement instead of saving your statements each month—if you prefer paper, you may want to file it in the Jan-Dec accordion file with paid bills, since it's a routine expense. If your closing documents are too large, you can archive them or store them on a bookshelf in a magazine holder, or store them in lateral file drawers perpendicularly alongside |

| File Content Category | Suggested Titles | Comments |
|---|---|---|
| | | the row of files. |
| Neighborhood Association | "(name of neighborhood/subdivision)" | Contains information about your neighborhood covenants and restrictions, a handbook or directory, pool and club information if applicable. |
| Personal Style | "Image" or "Hair Ideas" or "Fashion" or "Personal Style" | A place you can save clippings of fashion, hair and makeup ideas, if you have them. (Pinterest may be better for this info) |
| Pet Information | "(name of pet)," "Pet Info" | If you have more than one pet, you will probably want to name the folder by the pet's name. Contains vet bills and medical history, registration papers, pedigree, etc. |
| Property Taxes | "Property Tax" or "(name of street of your house)-Property Tax" | Keep each year's property tax statement and all related correspondence. It's good to keep them all together since you can look at them comparatively. |
| Restaurant Ideas | "Restaurants" or "Dining Out" | Ideas and clippings about restaurants you'd like to try, including that article of the "Ten Best Desserts" in your city, for example! (Can accomplish this electronically with Evernote.) |
| School | "(name of school)" | Can also keep this in your Family Binder—general information about school policies, student handbook. |

| File Content Category | Suggested Titles | Comments |
|---|---|---|
| Special Interests | Assign title according to interests, such as "Camping," "Parenting," "Waterskiing," "Genealogy," etc. | Contains articles of interest, notes from seminars about that subject, information about equipment you might need for it, etc. |
| Things to Do | "Things to Do" or "Travel-Local Places" or "Activities" or "Recreation" | Ideas and clippings about local/regional activities you and guests can do on a weekend or even day trips in your area. (Consider making a "Tourist Binder" for your guest room-- visit *clutterdiet.com/homeofficevideos* for a video I made about that.) |
| Travel | Try two main folders—"Travel- Places We've Been," and "Travel- Places We'd Like to Go" | Keep your ideas here for future travel, as well as saving brochures, maps, and directions for places you've been in case you want to go back or tell someone else about them. |
| Travel Reward Programs | "Frequent Flyer Programs" or "Mileage Programs" or "Travel Reward Programs" | Contains latest statements about your airline, hotel and rental car points. No need to keep past statements, just throw out the oldest one when you add a new one. You probably don't need separate folders for all of them. Also, strongly consider requesting paperless statements for these programs or a service like Manilla.com. |

| File Content Category | Suggested Titles | Comments |
| --- | --- | --- |
| Trophies | "Trophies-(name of person)" | An optional file that I like to call Trophies, but you can call it something else you like. It contains achievements you are particularly proud of, like an important thank-you note from a customer, an article about you in the newspaper, a copy of your first check received in your business, or a certificate for an award. |
| Warranties & Instructions | "Warranties- Appliances, Other"<br><br>"Warranties- Art & Décor"<br><br>"Warranties- Computer/Peripherals"<br><br>"Warranties- Furniture"<br><br>"Warranties- Jewelry"<br><br>"Warranties- Kids' Toys"<br><br>"Warranties- Kitchen"<br><br>"Warranties- Major Appliances"<br><br>"Warranties- Outdoor/Garage"<br><br>"Warranties- | These are suggested categories. If you don't have many warranties, you can get away with using a separate accordion file labeled with these categories to keep all of this together. Most homeowners find that they will use these as separate files. They can be reviewed and purged each time you access them.<br><br>For computer manuals and disks that came with your machine when you bought it, it's a good idea to bundle these together with a zippered plastic bag before filing to make sure you know which things go with which computer. Alternatively, you can store these computer items together in a binder case on a shelf, since they are often bulky. |

| File Content Category | Suggested Titles | Comments |
|---|---|---|
| | Personal/Health" | |
| | "Warranties- Small Electronics" | |
| | "Warranties- Sports & Exercise" | |
| | "Warranties- TV/DVD/DVR" | |

## What Do I Need to Keep, and For How Long?

This is one of the most commonly asked questions about paper management.

**You do need to check with your own accountant and/or attorney to be sure about your particular situation,** as retention requirements are complicated and depend greatly upon your industry and many other factors.

For tax-related documents, the general rule in the United States is that the IRS can go back as far as they want to investigate if they suspect fraud. However, **the guideline of keeping seven years of tax-supporting documentation is generally accepted by most accountants and other experts.**

Keep in mind that "tax-supporting" documentation refers to bank statements, receipts, and other less important tax paperwork, but it is recommended that you keep the actual tax return itself indefinitely. And anything related to purchases of investments like stocks or bonds needs to be kept if it helps you determine the original purchase price so that you can understand what your gain (or loss) is over time.

In general, there are only three reasons to keep any information:

1)      To document something for historical significance
2)      To protect yourself for possible legal or financial reasons
3)      To maintain useful, needed information for future use

To help you with some of these confusing retention questions, refer to the chart on the next page. **These suggestions are general guidelines compiled from several different sources, including attorneys, accountants, and organizing experts, but they are no substitute for your own consultation with your own accountant and/or attorney.**

## Paper Retention Guidelines Chart

Go to *clutterdiet.com/retention* for a printable reference PDF of this chart.

| Information | Suggested Length of Retention |
|---|---|
| Annual financial statements | Retain indefinitely |
| Automobile insurance | Statute of limitations, some say forever |
| Automobile registrations & titles | As long as you own the car |
| Bank reconciliations, statements, canceled & voided checks, checks stubs and check register tapes | 6-7 years |
| Birth certificates, citizenship papers or adoption papers, marriage & divorce papers, health & vaccination records, military records | Permanently |
| Canceled payroll and dividend checks | 6-7 years |
| Contracts | 3-7 years after completion |
| Copyrights, trademarks, and patents | Indefinitely or as long as in effect |
| Corporate documents | Permanently |
| Credit card statements and receipts | 6-7 years |
| Death certificates | Retain indefinitely |
| Disability insurance | Duration of policy |

| Information | Suggested Length of Retention |
|---|---|
| Fixed asset documents related to depreciation & values | Retain indefinitely |
| Health insurance | Duration of policy |
| Homeowners insurance | Statute of limitations, some say forever |
| Household inventory | Update annually |
| Housing records, such as home improvements, additions, buying & selling expenses | As long as you own the home, then with tax records |
| Income tax audit information, protests, court briefs and appeals | Retain indefinitely |
| Income tax returns and supporting documents | 6-7 years for tax-supporting documents, returns indefinitely |
| Investment purchase records | As long as you own the investment, then keep with sale record |
| IRA contribution & Social Security records | Permanently |
| Liability insurance | Statute of limitations, some say forever |
| Life insurance and umbrella policies | Duration of policy |

| Information | Suggested Length of Retention |
|---|---|
| Loan agreements | 6-7 years after completion of payment |
| Monthly financial statements used for internal purposes | 3 years |
| Passports | Keep current |
| Paycheck stubs | End of year until W-2 is confirmed, keep year-end statements |
| Pension plan records | Generally keep current year only |
| Personnel and payroll records, unemployment taxes and workers compensation insurance | Retain for four years |
| Purchase records, including purchase orders and vendor invoices | 6-7 years |
| Rental contracts | As long as in effect |
| Safe deposit box inventory | Update regularly |
| Sales records for investments | 6-7 years after sale, for tax purposes |
| Sales records such as invoices, monthly statements, remittance advisories, shipping papers, bill of lading and customers purchase orders | 6-7 years |
| Trust agreements | As long as in effect |

| Information | Suggested Length of Retention |
|---|---|
| Warranties, guarantees, receipts for major purchases, and instructions | As long as you own the items, some add 3 years |
| Wills and instructions, powers of attorney | Permanently, with regular updates |

## Arms' Length: Archiving Older Files

Archiving your files is a good practice, usually done once a year. Around tax time in April is a good time, since you are handling paper heavily and are finished with the previous calendar year of paperwork. You want your Handy reference files to be recent and relevant, making room for new things and keeping things pruned and manageable.

I like using bankers' boxes (cardboard boxes made specifically for archiving papers) if the papers will be stored indoors, or plastic file boxes for storage in attics or other less protected areas.

During this archiving process, anything that is not relevant or recent either gets shredded, recycled, or archived. **A good guideline is to keep dated items for the current and immediately previous year, and archive anything that is older.**

You can simply grab the folders from the drawer and place them in a box to be archived, or you can use large mailing envelopes (I like the 9 x 12" size) and transfer them from the folders to keep the papers from falling out and getting mixed up.

Label the outside of the envelopes appropriately before putting them into the box (I just use a permanent marker for this labeling because it's fast, and you're very likely to never look at this again).

**If you are using an alphabetical system, open a spreadsheet or word processing document and quickly make a list of every folder you are putting into boxes.** Keep the folders in alphabetical order in the boxes as you go. Then alphabetize the list when you're finished and label the boxes with the year and alphabetical range. (Such as 2012, A-L) If you wish, print the list and put it inside each box as an index. Save the document to your hard drive and refer to it before you have to climb into the attic!

If you have filed your papers in folders by year, such as "Bank Statements 2012," archiving will be much easier. You can quickly remove dated material without having to sort it.

**If you are using a numerical search filing system, archiving is a breeze!** In fact, even if you have been using a traditional alphabetical system for your file drawers, you can easily do a numerical system for your Arms' Length archives.

Use either Evernote or a spreadsheet to create a list of numbered boxes, and list everything that is in the boxes along with relevant keywords. Now you'll have boxes labeled "Archive 1," "Archive 2," "Archive 3" and so on, with a list of contents for each.

If you use Evernote, I recommend having a separate notebook called "Archives" and a separate note for each box. You can even annotate each note with an audio recording of your own narration of what is in the box or even take a photo of the contents, so you can add more detail along with your keywording. See your exclusive Evernote video training on your bonus tutorials page at *clutterdiet.com/homeofficevideos*.

Add whatever level of detail in your indexing that will allow you to get more clarity before you dig into those stacks of boxes. You'll search on your computer before you search physically in a cold basement or hot attic. Being able to go right to the exact place to find something is a true joy and a massive time-saver!

Here's an example of what your archive index documentation might be like:

| Box | Description | Keywords |
|-----|-------------|----------|
| Archive 1 | Client files from 2011 | Smith account, customers, clients, key accounts, client invoices, Jones, Washington, Bassett, Roman, Davis, ABC Corporation, Jefferson, Barnes |
| Archive 2 | Bank Statements 2012, Brokerage Statements 2012, Tax Return 2009, Tax Return 2008, Credit Card Statements 2009 | Financial, income taxes, investments, IRS, credit cards, Visa, Mastercard, American Express, Bank of America, Smith Barney, Morgan Stanley |

# ELECTRONIC INFORMATION

Just as with paper reference files, you have information you want to keep at your Fingertips, other things you want as Handy Reference, and other data you want archived at Arms' Length. This section explores these electronically, so if you want to read about keeping paper for reference, visit the Paper Reference chapter.

## Fingertips Reference

Your quick reference "Fingertips" information—information that you might call a "cheat sheet" or checklist in paper form—has a lot of great places to live electronically on your smartphone, laptop, desktop, or tablet. The next few sections will help you figure out what is best for you. (If you'd like to keep some of this information in paper form, refer to the previous chapter.)

### Evernote

"Hands down," my favorite tool for Fingertips information is Evernote, *www.evernote.com*.

I made just for you, the purchasers of this book, an exclusive 20 minute video training on how to use Evernote, with real data in a live application, not just screenshots. Watch it online on our video bonus page at *clutterdiet.com/homeofficevideos*!

I like Evernote so much for these reasons:

- ☑ **It's free.** A premium version exists which gives you faster image recognition, higher capacity, better sharing options, and no advertisements but you don't need to upgrade to premium to get a great deal of use from the service.
- ☑ **It's everywhere.** Evernote synchronizes continuously between its smartphone and tablet apps, its desktop application, and the cloud. You can log in and access your notes from any computer, easily work with your notes on your own laptop or desktop, and capture and access notes from your smartphone or tablet anywhere. I use it all of these places, most often on my tablet, laptop, and smartphone. You can

even designate some of your notebooks as offline so you can access them if you don't have an internet connection (for example, if you are traveling).

✓ **It's versatile.** You can use Evernote for everything from instructions and procedures to recipes and contact information. Right now we're talking about Fingertips information you want to have immediately handy, but later I'll explain how you can use Evernote for lots of other less immediate reference information.

✓ **It's beyond words, literally.** Apart from just text that you type or paste into your notes, you can also add photos and file attachments to notes and record audio narrations directly into a note.

✓ **It's searchable.** Your entire Evernote database is searchable and easy to filter, but even better… when you attach a photo or paste an image into a note, the text within that image becomes searchable! So if you take a picture of a frittata recipe from a magazine in a waiting room somewhere, later if you search "frittata" or even "eggs," that note will show up in the results. Snapping quick photos is a fast and easy way to "scan" something into your notes. I have snapped photos of handouts from presentations I have attended, and I have pasted screenshots from webinars and websites into my notes. All text searchable.

**For your Fingertips reference items, like cheat sheets, phone lists, soccer schedules, or anything else you want to look up fast when you need it, create a note for it in Evernote.** Tag it "Fingertips," or whatever you like, and make sure all relevant keywords that come to mind are present in the note text or tagged.

## Passwords & Other Sensitive Information

You may need sensitive information at your Fingertips too, but one type of Fingertips information you definitely *do not* want in Evernote is your passwords.

**Having a consistent system for keeping your passwords will prevent one of the biggest time-wasters I often witness!** Not having the right password at the right time can cause ridiculous delays and hassles. Am I right? Please capture your passwords as soon as you create or change them. **Just do it.**

Here are some dos and don'ts about passwords-- advice that we all need to follow, and this means YOU. I am privy to the password habits of many of my clients, and I know that even very smart people don't always practice these rules.

## THUMBS DOWN

- Don't put passwords on sticky notes on monitors!
- Don't store passwords written on paper under the glass on your desk surface!
- No Word doc or Excel file called "PASSWORDS" on the desktop
- No notebook lying around that says "PASSWORDS" on it
- Don't use the same password for everything
- Don't use passwords that are easy to guess, like birthdays, kids' names, etc.

## THUMBS UP

- Use more than one and keep them complicated and hard to crack
- Take special care with **VIPs: Very Important Passwords**
  - o Bank accounts
  - o Credit card accounts
  - o Email accounts (NOTE: Email is the most sacred VIP of all! Once someone has your email account they can get access to almost all of your others if a password reminder is sent via email.)
- Change VIPs periodically
- Make sure one or two other people close to you know how to get into your passwords and where they are stored
- Use strong passwords, especially for VIPs, meaning a combination of letters in upper and lower case and numbers and symbols
- Track your passwords in a secure place and have an immediate and consistent habit of documenting them as soon as you create or change them

**Electronic ways to store passwords:**

The best advantage of an electronic password keeper? Having only one password to unlock them all! I love not having to remember anything else.

I have used SplashID for years, moving my database from device to device, all the way back from having a Handspring Treo on a Palm platform to my current super nifty Android phone. This software is available for almost all platforms and synchronizes securely between your smartphone and desktop, enabling you to have your information safely with you out and about.

I am loyal and very accustomed to using SplashID, but there are many other good ones, some possibly better depending upon your preferences. LastPass, Password Depot, Password Agent, and many others are available and do a great job.

**Remember that you can capture other account information here too, not just logins and passwords.** Here are some things I like storing in my password keeper database:

- ☑ Credit card numbers
- ☑ Bank account information
- ☑ Magazine subscription info
- ☑ Software licenses
- ☑ Identification numbers (SSN, Drivers License numbers of drivers in my family)
- ☑ Gate codes
- ☑ Safe and padlock combinations
- ☑ Frequent customer numbers
- ☑ Travel awards program information

If you insist upon having a physical method for storing your passwords, these are the two best methods:

- **A-Z card file.** Get an index card file box and write information for each account on a card, filing them alphabetically.
- **An unused, old-fashioned address book or the Internet Password Organizer book.** (*clutterdiet.com/internetpasswordorganizer*) Write in your password information on the alphabetized pages. These solutions are basically the same, but the Internet Password Organizer works better because it is made for this purpose, with fields labeled in a way that makes sense for this use. If you use this book method, use a pencil to mark your entries so that you can erase as things change.

**Either way, you may consider writing your entries in code in case your book or card file is lost or stolen.** For example, if your password is your first pet's name plus your graduation year, like Fido1991, you might write down "first pet + year" as a clue for yourself.

## Handy Reference: Electronic Documents

Filing your "Handy Reference" electronic documents is getting easier all the time, with newer cloud resources and better search capabilities. But the basics still are important, no matter what tool you use.

- ☑ **Group like files and documents together into folders.** Making sense of large numbers of loose documents is difficult at best.

- ☑ **Name things intelligently.** Don't name files and folders with vague words like "Miscellaneous," "Stuff," or "Info." How will you think about finding this later? Will you remember the names of everyone involved, or the name of the occasion? What will be relevant to you next time you anticipate looking for this item?

- ☑ **Use consistent naming conventions for files and folders.** In other words, name all similar things in a similar way. For example, folders for photos can be named with the month and year of the occasion, done in this format: YYYY-MM [Month] [Name of Occasion]
    - o For example: "2010-07 July Kermit's Wedding." If you use this naming convention for all of your photo folders, your folders will line up like this screenshot you see here.

- 2011-01 January
- 2011-01 January LA Organizing Awards
- 2011-02 February
- 2011-03 March
- 2011-04 April
- 2011-05 May
- 2011-06 June
- 2011-07 July
- 2011-07 July New York with boys
- 2011-08 August
- 2011-09 September
- 2011-10 October- Reese- Korey Howell
- 2011-10 October-General
- 2011-11 November EIA
- 2011-11 November-General
- 2011-12 December

☑ **Use consistent naming conventions for stages of revisions and versions.** When passing a document between various parties for revisions using Word's Track Changes options or other reviewing tools, save and name the file consistently so that you can more readily tell which version is newest. For example, if you send a file to Wendy for her changes, she can save the new version as "2012-11-10 Wendy's changes-DRAFT-XYZ Proposal." When rounds of changes are completed, name the file "FINAL" in front of the regular file name you chose, such as "FINAL-XYZ Proposal."

☑ **Better yet, put shared documents in the cloud.** The problem of versions as described in the previous paragraph can be avoided if all participants in the review have access to the same actual document. Tools like Dropbox, SugarSync, and Google Docs/Google Drive make it easy for people to collaborate, saving tons of time and confusion. Dropbox has been a lifesaver for our office, which is entirely virtual. Our team members can effortlessly share files and folders and we're all working from the same set of information. With Dropbox, we also have our information everywhere we go, even offline. This capability means I can work even on an airplane (without Wi-Fi) with my actual data, and it synchronizes with the rest of my information when I next connect to the internet. Dropbox also has a lovely "Camera Uploads" feature, which grabs every photo you take with your smartphone or tablet and instantly uploads it to your Dropbox folder, accessible from any other device you have. Genius!

☑ **Backups are essential! It's not a matter of if your hard drive will fail; it's WHEN.** Even if you have documents in the cloud, you still may feel better having a regular backup elsewhere. And there may be larger files that you don't put in the cloud at all, such as music and photos, which definitely need backing up too. I have always liked Carbonite and Mozy, which both do excellent jobs of automating and securing your backup files at a very affordable cost.

☑ **To force important folders to the top of an alphabetical list, use a symbol like the + (plus) sign.** You can choose a different symbol, but I like the plus sign because it symbolizes more importance. You can even use two or more symbols to continue to force the alphabetical order if the folders still don't cooperate, as seen in this screenshot example. I access the files for my business more than any other folder on my hard drive, so I want that to always appear at the top of the list so I can get to it quickly, no matter what the name of the folder is.

- ++Primary Folder
- +Another primary folder
- A normal folder
- Beekeeping
- Carpet cleaning
- Dirt biking
- Elephant riding
- Fishing
- Gasoline consumption
- Hamburgers

## Your Computer Desktop

Does your desktop look like this?

**In terms of clutter, think of your computer desktop** *just like* **your physical desk top!** It's the first thing you see when you sit down to work, so make sure it reflects the same calm and focused environment you'd like to see in your physical space.

**Desktops are like a dashboard of your frequently used tools. Think again about your actual desk.** Where do you want your phone, your pens, your recycling basket, your stack of sticky notes? Think about what frequently used tools, folders, and documents you need to use and position them accordingly.

You want your desktop to be a temporary holding place for new and necessary things you want in front of you, just as you would on your desk, and **you do** *not* **want to use your desktop for storage.**

**A note about desktop icons, specifically for Windows users:**
I want to make sure you know the difference between a shortcut and an actual document or folder. A shortcut is an icon that has a small arrow on it, indicating that clicking it is actually accessing a document, folder, or executable program that is located elsewhere. See the illustration on the next page:

**This arrow indicates that clicking here takes you to the actual location of the folder somewhere else.**       **This folder does not have an arrow, so the folder itself actually resides on the desktop.**

Knowing this, we want to make sure that we don't delete actual files and folders when we are meaning to delete a shortcut to them.

**Think about our A-B-C-D prioritization of storage with your desktop** (see Workspace chapter for a full explanation). Basically, you want to have your most frequently used items in the most accessible spaces.

Speaking mainly of Windows environments, your A-B-C-D prioritization looks like this:

| Items | Priority | Place |
|---|---|---|
| Most frequently needed icons/shortcuts | A | Taskbar (on side or at bottom, with most used program and folder icons—visible at all times) |
| Slightly less frequently needed icons/shortcuts | B | Desktop and/or Start menu (think of the Start menu like a "drawer" of your desk—one more step to open and access than the taskbar) |
| Rarely or sometimes used programs (don't need a shortcut icon for them) | C | "All programs" menu from within the Start menu |
| Unused icons/shortcuts/ documents | D | DELETE or DRAG to another folder! You're not using it, or you need to store it elsewhere away from the desktop itself. |

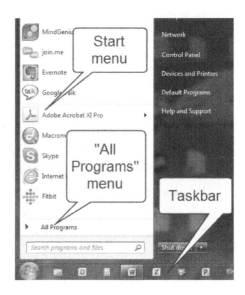

Place your shortcuts and tools according to this framework for daily efficiency.

## Evernote for Handy Reference

Earlier in this chapter we introduced and explained Evernote in terms of Fingertips reference information, and I wanted to give you some ideas for how to use Evernote for lots of other Handy information you don't necessarily need to have at your Fingertips.

Here are some of the kinds of information that people keep in Evernote:

- Gift ideas (also can use a secret board on Pinterest for this purpose)
- Phone and meeting notes (Typing up whatever is discussed in meetings to keep for reference later, keywording and tagging with the appropriate companies, clients, or people's names)
- Recipes (use tags for categories of food like Soups, Salads, Entrees, Desserts, etc.)
- Contact information (check out the Evernote add-on app called *Hello*, for documenting your relationships with contacts)
- Books you might want to read
- Movies you might want to see
- Music you might want to buy
- Restaurants you might want to try
- Wines you want to remember and buy again
- Book notes for key points of what you want to recall when reading (paste in an image of the book cover for better recall of the book)
- Random tips people tell you for apps, websites, investment ideas, etc.
- Articles you want to keep
- Handouts you receive from presentations—snap a photo of the pages with your handwritten notes on them, tag the note, and toss the paper
- Anything you want to paste and save from the web for later—Evernote automatically notes the URL it originates from so you can go back to it later (also, use the Evernote add-on app called *Clearly* to get rid of clutter on web pages before copying and pasting)

## *Arms' Length: Archiving Older Files*

I don't believe in spending too much time deleting old files. Memory space is cheap, certainly cheaper than the value of your time! If there are obvious things, then yes, delete them... but you don't typically need to open up everything and examine it to decide whether to keep it, etc. If files are old and in your way, archive them to a DVD or an external hard drive or move them to a folder where they won't be distracting. (As always, in matters of file retention, please consult your attorney or accountant for more definitive answers about your situation and your industry.)

## Software & Hardware

Software can be very expensive, costing hundreds of dollars. Losing a license number or unlock code can be very painful and frustrating! Make a new habit of capturing all software purchase information as soon as you buy it. You can use a spreadsheet that we have free for you on our Free Tips page on our website (see the left side list of downloads at *clutterdiet.com/freetips*), or you can use a password database like SplashID to track it, since often there is also a login involved.

There are three kinds of software found in home offices:

1. **Purchased in a box.** Inside this big box usually is a manual, some sheets of paper, and one or two DVDs. These boxes are just boxes of air, taking up space on a shelf. All you need is the contents, which can be stored in CD/DVD wallets saving many linear feet of shelf space! Find these wallets (Case Logic is a good brand) at any discount store or office supply store. You can fit literally over 100 discs in a few inches of space.
2. **Provided with a new PC.** Use plastic document cases, found at office supply stores, to easily store together on a shelf all of the manuals, warranty papers, and backup software that comes with a new computer.
3. **Downloaded.** Most software is now purchased by direct download online, meaning you need to remember where you bought it, ideally keep the install file handy, and save the license information. I keep an Install Files folder on my desktop and have a habit of putting all new downloaded software there. If I ever need to reinstall something, I know exactly where to find it.

**Can't remember your software license numbers or how much RAM you have?** Getting your computer fixed often means you're answering a lot of questions from a technician that seem overwhelming. To help with this, and in case of a hard drive failure, I periodically take a "snapshot" of my computers with Belarc Advisor (*Belarc.com*, look for the free download version). This software produces a very helpful printed report whenever you like. A list is generated of all of the hardware, how much memory I have, all of the important technical specs, and all of the software that is installed. It even lists the license numbers for most of the software!

# EMAIL

We featured a chapter on Electronic Information, but I deliberately did not include email within that content, as it deserves its own chapter entirely.

**The two biggest complaints I hear from people are about paper and email. Why do you think that is the case?**

Both paper and email represent communications that require many decisions and actions. **They are both paralyzing and overwhelming, and they both keep coming, whether in the physical mailbox or the electronic inbox.** You are forced to continue dealing with a relentless stream of these decisions.

Since this is not going to stop anytime soon, what you need are strategies for making these decisions quickly and not letting the processing of all of it consume your day. **The more time you spend processing, the less time you can spend being truly productive.**

## *When to Check Your Email*

First, a moment for me to be a heretic again. **It's quite popular now in our industry of organizing and productivity to give the firm advice not to check email first thing in the morning. I really have to disagree with that,** and I'm sorry because some of the people who say this the most are friends of mine.

But I think the distinction is in the approach. **There is a huge difference between "checking" email and "processing" email.** To me, checking means quickly seeing what has come through and noting anything that might be an urgent matter that needs attention. Processing means "doing" your email—replying, getting sucked in.

There are several reasons why I have been glad I *checked* my email in the morning:

- Someone has cancelled on a meeting or client appointment for that day
- Someone needs to reschedule a time or postpone something a few minutes
- My website is down and I get an automated notification email about that
- When I was managing my team of organizers out in the field, a client has cancelled his/her appointment, meaning if we didn't know, someone on my team would be out driving someplace for no reason
- A media person wants to talk to me and she is on deadline (yes, this does happen, which is cool)
- Someone is waiting on a quick question to be answered from me to continue their own work that morning

**Absolutely, when this advice is given about not checking, it has to do with being proactive vs. reactive in your work habits, and I agree with being proactive as much as possible.** Realities of the world and the workplace do mean that we do have urgencies to contend with, depending upon the type of job we have and the level of responsibility we carry. The key is not letting those urgencies control us entirely.

You decide how often you need to process your email vs. "check" your email… but for most people, three times a day is sufficient for checking email, and the challenge is to stop yourself from getting sucked into other people's agendas and stick with your own. **I recommend doing a few quick checks and saving the heavy processing for once or twice a day,** meaning that is when to decide "Action, Reference, or Trash?" and really clear out your inbox.

> YOUR INBOX IS A CONVENIENT ORGANIZING SYSTEM FOR OTHER PEOPLE'S AGENDAS.
>
> - Brendon Burchard

**Checking email on your smartphone is a clever way to avoid getting consumed with replies,** since it's usually much harder to type lengthy responses when you have to peck them out with your fingers on a tiny keyboard. You can also easily delete things before they ever reach your actual inbox and clutter it up.

In my Clutter Diet® online program, we have a lot of fun with the metaphor of weight loss as applied to your home. **One of the biggest parallels between weight loss and getting** organized is that they both require Prevention, Reduction, and Maintenance for long term success. So let's explore how we can cut your email calories and shed some pounds of stress!

## Prevention

- ✓ **Unsubscribe to as much as you can, and better yet, don't subscribe in the first place.** (Unless it's my newsletter ☺) Make sure the content is really adding value to your life, is consistent with your goals and objectives, and is not just a constant sales pitch. Take an extra moment to unsubscribe instead of just hitting delete—it's a tiny investment of time that will pay off.

- ✓ **Be careful when you buy something online**—make sure the checkbox for receiving other communications from the vendor, and especially from "their partners," is not checked off by default. **Check privacy policies** to make sure you understand how your information is going to be used.

- ✓ **Make sure your IT person has helped you set up the best spam filtering you can get for your particular situation.** Spam is a terrible time-waster!

- ✓ **Have conversations with significant email senders in your life** about your desire to reduce your e-mail.
  - o **Individuals:** You can agree for someone like an assistant to send you a report in digest form of several issues and events that have occurred in one day, vs. sending you an individual e-mail about each item. And if you are on someone's "joke list," ask politely to be removed as you are trying to prevent inbox overload. Most people will understand.
  - o **Teams/Departments:** Have deliberate, facilitated conversations about what could be done about reducing e-mail in your company culture. Some companies are experimenting with "No E-mail Fridays" to encourage people to pick up the phone and interact more, and to have more focused, productive time. Talk to your team about who really needs to copy whom and find out if there are obvious things that can be changed-- the only way to know is to talk about it directly.

- ✓ **Remember, the more email you send, the more you will get.** Are your emails really necessary? Are you the culprit in ultimately creating more email for yourself?

☑ **Prevent interruptions by shutting off email alerts, both on your main computer and your smartphone.** If you want to stay in control of your email and be proactive, you need to stop allowing signals that continue to force you to be reactive. *You decide* when to check your email instead of letting alerts pop up and constantly tell you messages have arrived.

## *Reduction*

**Think of your email inbox as being the same as your physical mailbox out by the curb.** Do you go out there and check it a few times a day, open a couple of envelopes and read them, stuff them back inside, then leave all of the mail in there and go back in the house, letting it pile up day after day? Of course not.

So start keeping the inbox pared down. Some colleagues of mine have taught people the concept of "Inbox Zero," and that is certainly ideal. This concept means that you are leaving your computer at the end of each day with literally no messages in your inbox— they have all been filed away in folders or pending actions in Tasks.

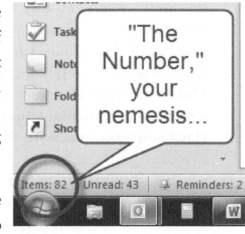

I think instead that sometimes it would actually take longer to process a message as a Task than it would to leave the email in your inbox for a quick answer the next day. And some days you just can't get to all of it before it's time to close up shop.

**Because of that I really believe it's better to pick a "Happy Number" of inbox messages that makes you feel happy and relieved when you see it.** For me, that number is 20 or fewer. For others, it could be 50 or 100. What might be a good indicator is the number of emails you can easily see on your screen without scrolling. **Each day, work toward leaving your desk with your Happy Number of messages (or lower) in your inbox.** Doing this takes focus, but you can do it!

**Experiment with sorting your inbox different ways to see if it makes it easier to delete and process en masse.** For example, sorting by sender can allow you to see a thread of messages and realize you need only respond to the last one in the thread. You also might see that something common like all of your Facebook notifications are grouped together, and you can hit delete quickly as you read them all in a row. Sorting by date received can help you see what is more recent and urgent.

## Quick Relief: Do an Email Knockdown

I have seen it many, many times that people have literally thousands of emails in their inboxes. **To knock it down to a manageable size fast, pick a reasonable date in the recent past by which you are 99% certain anything before that date has been handled or followed up with further emails.**

**For example, if it's February, you might pick January 1st, or December 1st... and any messages prior to that date get archived into a folder.** You still have them, they are searchable, and everything is going to be okay! But they will be out of your inbox and you can get closer to that fresh start. **NOW look at that inbox number! Less intimidating?**

**Next, use rules and folders to start weeding out and organizing what is left.** In Outlook 2010, Rules are on the Home ribbon, and older versions may have it under Tools> Rules & Alerts (or even "Rules Wizard"). On other platforms, these rules may be called "filters."

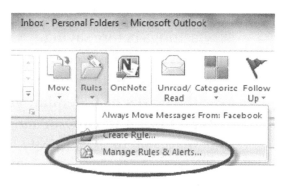

**You can set up rules like these:**
- Anything from a certain sender or with a certain subject line keyword can be set up to automatically go to a specific folder, so maybe routine newsletters can go to a folder you call "Read/Review," taking them out of your daily processing.
- Anything from a certain sender or with specific keywords can be listed as a certain color in your inbox, or flagged a certain way. (For example, emails from your boss can be turned red in the list.)

✓ Anything from a certain sender (like your manager or your spouse) can be set to pop up an alert when it appears, even if general alerts are turned off.

✓ Anything you want can be automatically forwarded, deleted, or moved to a specific folder based on the parameters you specify.

In Outlook, you may need to click "Run Rules Now" the first time you set this up. You'll be very surprised at all of the things rules and filters can do!

**Next, use our Action-Reference-Trash (A-R-T) decision technique to help you quickly plow through the remainder of the inbox.** (See our chapter on Processing Information for more detail.)

✓ **ACTION means you need to do something with that message—** respond, read/review, research, delegate, etc. You can leave these in your inbox if they are quick, or you can use Outlook tasks and calendar functions to drag the messages and create tasks and appointments from them.

    o **If you left-click and drag a message with your mouse to the Tasks or Calendar, the text from that message will be pasted into the notes field** of the Task or Appointment, where you can edit the subject and fix other settings before saving.

    o **If you right-click and drag a message with your mouse to the Tasks or Calendar, you get an option to copy or move the message in its entirety, as an attachment,** into a new Task or Appointment. I usually prefer this method, since I can act upon the message with a full set of menu options like Reply and Forward, and I don't have to locate the message again.

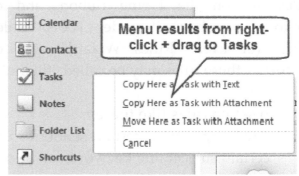

✓ **REFERENCE means no action is required, but you need to keep it on file for later—so get it out of the inbox.** Create a system of folders that works for you to go back and find things quickly. It could be one folder called "General Reference," or you could have folders for various parts of your job and life. Don't make so many folders that the decision-making slows you down! Keep it simple. Remember, it's all searchable and sortable. Typically we try to set up as few folders as possible.

☑ **TRASH means hitting the DELETE key.** But before hitting delete, always ask yourself if you can unsubscribe to that particular type of message first and do that too.

Keep going with Action-Reference-Trash as your guiding question, until you've processed through your inbox to your satisfaction, your "Happy Number." And now your Tasks and Appointments will be your guide as to what actions are required and when.

## *Maintenance*

☑ **Process your email regularly with the A-R-T decision-making technique, and target that "Happy Number" daily.** If you can achieve it only once a week, you're still better off than you were feeling before.

☑ As you maintain, always keep Prevention in mind. Unsubscribe as you can and keep those principles in practice.

☑ As referenced above, you want to manage email, not have it manage you. As you maintain your inbox, use these practices to help you stay proactive:

   o **Check and process your emails at certain designated points of the day, not continuously.** If you are trying to get productive work done, email will be a constant interruption if you let it.

   o **If you are finding yourself addicted to pressing the Send/Receive button and are constantly interrupting yourself to check email, STOP.** *Ask yourself what you are avoiding and why.* You may discover that simply being aware of this habit stops it, or you may need to get some accountability from someone else to help you stick to what you'd rather be working on.

   o **If you simply must check your email, glance at your smartphone instead of getting into Outlook or Gmail on a bigger screen.** You can see and respond if anything urgent has arrived and delete anything you can, otherwise you may be tempted to do more than check.

## LORIE'S PRODUCTIVITY PROVERB:

I will improve my productivity when I **manage** the distractions I cannot control; **stop allowing** the distractions I do control; and **stay present** enough to know the difference.

# CONTACTS

Managing your relationships today is certainly more complicated than it used to be. People have multiple email addresses, social media accounts and phone numbers, and an old handwritten address book just doesn't cut it anymore!

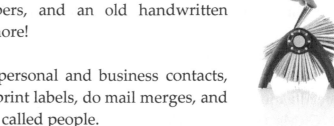

Most people need separate sets of personal and business contacts, and they usually need the ability to print labels, do mail merges, and print a quick phone list of frequently called people.

**This ability to manage and print various formats of your contact records won't work very well if they are not entered in the first place!** Most home offices I've seen have a large stack of rubber-banded business cards, or even a drawer or box full of them.

## *Managing Contacts in Paper Form*

**If you don't have very many business cards and don't need to print the information or manage it digitally, a card file system is the most efficient handwritten format,** in my opinion. You can write all you want on an index card or Rolodex card with plenty of space, and you can fasten a business card directly to the card instead of re-writing everything. Then if the contact moves or changes information, you can start a fresh new card instead of trying to erase inside a book.

If you have a small collection of business cards that are specific to something like a remodeling project or you otherwise need to carry them around physically, **there are business card "wallets" or "folios" available at office supply stores,** which are booklets with pages of plastic sleeves in them that you can easily flip through and rearrange as needed. You can also assemble your own 3-ring binder with inserted business card plastic sleeves, also available at office supply stores.

## Managing Contacts Digitally

While some can manage their contacts effectively in paper form, most people do need to find an electronic contact management system for more robust needs.

**For typical home office needs, you'll want to choose an application that can synchronize with your smartphone, such as Google Contacts, Outlook, or Apple's iCloud.** You can have your information with you everywhere you go, and it will be backed up too, unlike a lost paper address book where there is no way to recover it.

**If you need a more sales-oriented contact management system for your business, you can look at CRMs (Customer Relationship Managers) like Sage ACT! or Salesforce.com.** Industry-specific CRMs also are common, such as special systems for real estate agents or Mary Kay consultants, for example. Usually these are going to be the best for your needs, since they are custom built for what you do. Ask others in your industry what they use and get a sense of what's available before deciding.

## Capturing Contact Information

**Make a policy for yourself that you are committed to capturing contact information as you use it and need it.** Don't rely on asking someone else for it (your spouse, assistant, etc.) or think that you'll use it just this one time—go ahead and enter the person into your system right away. It's better to not need it later and have it, than to need it later and *not* have it. I believe that keeping up with your own contact information is a responsibility of every adult person, kind of like you are responsible for keeping your car filled with gas or keeping your pet fed.

**When you receive new business cards or other bits of contact information (like a return address torn from an envelope), put them somewhere on or near your desk as a dedicated spot for later data entry.** A small basket will do nicely, or you can put them in a tray or dish or anything else you want to use.

**As you place things into your data entry basket, make notes on them so you can more easily remember details about each person.** Group cards from events with a paper clip or rubber band, and add a sticky note to remember the name of the event (such as "April NSA Chapter Meeting").

## Entering Contact Information

**When you encounter information within an email message, such as someone's email signature, make a habit of quickly copying and pasting that information into a new contact record.** If you are using Outlook, you can right-click on the person's address in the message and choose "Add to Outlook Contacts."

**If you frequently need to add information to your contacts from email signatures and such, there is a terrific application called "Address Grabber."** (*egrabber.com*) This software allows you to highlight and click once to intelligently grab information wherever you find it and parse it into the correct fields of your contact record. It saves people so much time and works like a charm!

**For the business cards you've collected in your data entry basket, you have several great options:**

- ✓ **CardScan.** These scanners work surprisingly well for processing stacks of cards quickly. The software allows you to save an image of the card along with the data it pulls from the scan. You'll want to verify each for accuracy, you sometimes will need to re-type a number or two, and then click save. Much faster than entering them all the long way.

- ✓ **There are apps for this.** WorldCard Mobile, CardMunch, and others are available on your smartphone. A desktop scanner is easier for a higher volume of cards, but these work well, especially if you want to enter a few of them right in the airport after a meeting.

- ✓ **Scanning services.** CloudContacts and Shoeboxed are very affordable services for scanning in your business cards (Shoeboxed also does receipts). You can mail them in or upload an image. CloudContacts will do both fronts and backs of cards and will include your handwritten notes in the final result!

- ☑ **Friendly neighborhood teenager data entry.** If you know a responsible babysitter-type person who wants to enter or scan cards for you at an hourly rate, that can also be a very affordable and smart way to save some time. Find someone on a neighborhood group or bulletin board. You might even get this person to run errands and do other tasks for you too!

**Some people use Evernote for managing their contact records.** If your needs are simple, you can take a photo of someone's business card within Evernote and its text will be searchable, and you can tag each note to create categories of contacts. Evernote's add-on module, called, "Hello," is a very interesting option that involves your taking a photo of people you meet face-to-face and logging other details about how you met.

**As you enter information, put keywords in the notes field of the contact record so that you make it searchable if you forget their names.** For example, you will probably not remember your plumber's given name, but you will remember the word "plumber," and you can search that term to find him. Think about how you would "Google" your own contacts.

**Always put in more than just contact information if you have it.** Details like birthdays, children's and spouse's names, pets' names, etc. are very helpful. You can also add any documentation about when you last spoke, where you met, or who introduced you. If you use Outlook, it has special fields for entering birthdays and anniversaries that make those occasions magically show up in your calendar!

**Categories are very helpful if you want to separate and sort groups of people within one larger database.** Most contact management applications make this relatively easy, so that you can separate business from personal, colleagues from clients, and so on. As you enter information, select this category as part of your process. Avoid having too many categories as it can slow down your decision-making and thus your progress. Keep it simple.

## *Maintaining Your Database*

**As you refer to your contacts and search within your database, stop and correct or delete as you see things that need attention.** And when someone notifies you of a change in contact information, make that change right away. Doing it in the moment takes only a few seconds and can save many minutes later!

**Sending annual mailings like holiday cards is very helpful as a prompt to clean up your database**, and receiving cards from others is a good verification tool to make sure you've got updated information. For that reason, right after the holidays is a terrific time to sit down and do some data entry, with all of the holiday envelopes in front of you.

**Got duplicates?** Sometimes with synchronization problems you may accidentally end up with duplicate entries for many or all of your contacts. Don't despair! Use "undupe" software. Do a Google search for "duplicates" with whatever your platform may be ("duplicates in Outlook," for example), and you will likely find more than one software solution or other fix for the problem.

**Lastly, no discussion of contacts is complete without this warning: Please make sure you are backing up your mobile phone data!** I have heard way too many stories of people keeping everything in their phones and suddenly losing it all when the phone is damaged or stolen. Either synchronize your phone with an online application, or get a backup application on your phone itself.

# FAMILY + HOME

Whether you work for yourself, for a company, or as a stay-at-home parent, a home office will always include the business of running a home. Doing the administrative work of any household requires significant planning, and it generates lots of paper and information, especially if you have children.

## *Sunday Planning*

> I am starting this chapter with an urgent plea for you to adopt this one habit above all others! If you were to do this ONE thing out of this entire book, I assert it would change your family life more than anything else.

**Take just 15-20 minutes to plan your week for your family.** I think that Sundays are typically ideal for this, since most people follow a Monday-Friday work schedule and have children's activities on Saturdays. Sundays are more often reserved for down time. If another day works better for you, do it then, but I refer to this habit as "Sunday Planning."

Here are the five things to consider as you sit down for Sunday Planning each week:

- **CALENDAR:** Review the calendar for everyone
- **CARPOOL:** Who is taking whom where, and when?
- **COOKING:** What's for dinner each evening? What do we need to buy to prepare it?
- **CHORES:** Who is cooking, cleaning, and doing dishes?
- **CHILDREN:** Is there a sitter required later in the week? Who is in charge of homework help? Who is doing bath and bedtime duty for younger children?

You'll need some paper or a tablet, your and your spouse's calendars, your recipe book, a grocery list, and probably your Family Binder (see next section). But if you don't have access to all of that, do it anyway, with just one sheet of paper and a pen... doing any of this is better than not doing it at all. You can even do a version of this in the car on the way to visit family or attend a worship service.

**You'll end up with peace of mind, meals planned for the week, a grocery list to buy or delegate, and ownership of some of the regular responsibilities that cause so much tension around the home.** You will thank yourself over and over!

**Author Brian Tracy says for every minute you spend planning, you save TEN!** That's a return on investment that is a winner over almost any other investment you can name.

# *Family Binder*

Next let's corral some of the paperwork. The Family Binder is "Command Central" for all of the commonly-needed Fingertips Reference information in your home.

**All you need is a large 3-ring binder and some sturdy dividers, preferably with pockets.** Office supply stores do sell extra-wide dividers now that will easily stick out beyond page protector sheets, so you might also look for that feature.

Other options for the binder are sheet protectors for important pages, business card holders to keep frequently-called vendors' cards handy, and a zippered pouch to hold pens, sticky notes, and other supplies.

**Below are some suggested categories and ideas for things you can put in your binder.**

## Administration/Activities

- ☑ Frequently called numbers page with emergency numbers on it
- ☑ Family master calendar
- ☑ Family phone directory (can print out your Outlook address book for reference)
- ☑ Phone lists for various organizations and classes
- ☑ Schedules for activities such as sports and clubs
- ☑ School holiday calendar

☑ Wish Lists for books to read and videos to rent

## Child Care

☑ Sitter reference information (meals, snacks, naps, rules)
☑ Carpool and day care information
☑ Time sheets for sitters or nannies
☑ Petty cash account tracking sheet for sitters or nannies
☑ Task list for sitters or nannies

## Cleaning & Maintenance

☑ Cleaning schedules and checklists
☑ Indoor maintenance checklists
☑ Outdoor maintenance checklists
☑ Light bulb chart
☑ Car VIN numbers and license plate numbers
☑ Car maintenance records
☑ Recycling and trash service reference information
☑ Storage inventory lists
☑ Home inventory information

## Events & Holidays

☑ Perpetual birthday calendar (list of all birthdays regardless of year)
☑ Birthday party checklist
☑ Entertaining checklist
☑ Holiday card list
☑ Holiday planning notes
☑ Wish lists for holidays and birthdays
☑ Gift ideas list
☑ Clothing sizes

## Health & Safety

☑ Map to nearest hospital
☑ Medical insurance information
☑ Vaccination records

- ☑ Medical information and treatment permission forms for sitters
- ☑ Allergy and other important health information
- ☑ Pets' health information

## Meals

- ☑ Menu planning forms
- ☑ School lunch menu
- ☑ List of favorite breakfasts
- ☑ List of favorite school lunches
- ☑ List of favorite dinners
- ☑ Rotation menu for dinners
- ☑ List of meals in the freezer to use

## Travel

- ☑ Packing lists
- ☑ Leaving town checklist
- ☑ Camping checklist
- ☑ Picnic/outdoor events checklist
- ☑ "Places We'd Like to Go" list
- ☑ House sitter and pet sitter information

# *School Papers*

Sometimes the most challenging inflow of paper is the school stuff that invades the house every afternoon, spewing out of backpacks, binders, and tote bags.

There are four kinds of school papers, and for fun, we're going to have them all start with A so you can remember them more easily. **Make straight A's on managing your school papers!**

- ☑ **ACTION: Do**
  - ○ Forms, checks, permission slips, and homework are all Action papers—things you need to do. Separate those out immediately

as you find them so you can make sure they get done.

✓ **ARCHIVE: Keep**

   o These reference papers don't require any immediate action. They may be needed for future reference, so you can keep them in your Family Binder, your reference files, or your keepsakes bins.

✓ **AMBIGUOUS: Park**

   o Sometimes nobody really knows whether to keep a school paper or not. Already graded essays, unfinished worksheets, and handouts of various sorts… does the teacher want them back? Has the grade been counted? Is this incomplete work? Establish a parking spot for the "I Don't Know" papers so they can wait for further insight or instruction. One stacking paper tray for each child is a good container, and when the tray is full, that's your cue to clean it out and recycle what you can.

✓ **ARTWORK: Enjoy**

   o Have a gallery set up for prolific artists to show off their latest work—something beyond the refrigerator door! Designating a wall with a simple ribbon clothesline is an easy and inexpensive way to display current masterpieces. When new artwork comes along, you can make decisions about which ones to keep long term.

## Artwork

**Artwork seems to be the most challenging of these four types of school papers.** Some kids seem to produce more than others, and it can be difficult to discard it if your child's feelings get hurt or if you are a very sentimental person.

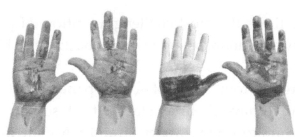

**If possible, have your child participate in the decision-making process.** You might be surprised at what items are important to them for various reasons.

**If you like, take a photo of each drawing or painting before discarding it.** You can also use the nifty *Artkive* app to take the photos, which allows you to make coffee mugs or books out of your collection of photos.

**When you keep something, make a note on the back if possible as to the date, the child's name and age, and any relevant information the child shared about what he or she created.** For example, the back of a drawing might say, "December 1999, Susie, age 4, Choo Choo Train."

**For keepsakes in general, we recommend having a "limiting container." Choose a bin that seems like an adequate size for your storage needs and habits, and then make a policy for yourself that this container is the limit for your memorabilia.** When you want to place new items into the bin, if they won't fit, it's time to prioritize and discard if you want to keep them. You decide what this limit is—whether you have space for one bin per school year, or just one bin per child—that is up to you. But stick to your policy once you've decided, especially if you tend to keep every scribble.

**If you need a larger container, check an art supply store for a portfolio, or make one yourself.** Instructions can be found online for making cardboard or poster board portfolios for larger paintings and drawings. Large portfolios can be stored behind or under furniture to get them out of the way.

## Recipes

The 3x5" card file your grandmother used to keep just isn't going to cut it nowadays! We are constantly printing recipes we find online or clipping them out of magazines in strange sizes. **I find the best way to manage recipes is with a 3-ring binder.**

**If you have lots of recipes, you may possibly need separate binders for desserts, main dishes, and so on.** But experience tells me that most people don't have that many recipes they actually have tried and have continued to use regularly.

**If you have a tendency to accumulate new recipes to try, don't mix them into your recipe binder until they are considered "keepers."** Have a separate accordion file or basket to keep new recipes separated until you try them first.

Here's how to put your binder together:

- ✓ Purchase a binder that is very sturdy with reinforced edges and room to grow. And ideally, find one with pockets on the inside of the covers.
- ✓ Use a combination of full-page sheet protectors and 3-ring photo sleeves (3x5" or 4x6" or a combination) to hold the recipes inside the binder. Using sleeves enables quick additions of new recipes without needing to punch holes, and the sleeves also protect the pages from splatters while you are cooking.
- ✓ Purchase tabbed dividers that are extra wide, so that the tabs extend beyond the edges of the sheet protectors. (Avery #11222 is an example of these.)
- ✓ Use these recommended categories, or create your own: Appetizers & Beverages, Breads & Breakfasts, Cakes/Pies/Desserts, Candy/Cookies, Main Dishes, Salads/Side Dishes, Sauces/Spices, Soups, Take Out Menus.

You can use the front inside pocket for new recipes you want to try, menu planning pages, or other notes. The back inside cover pocket can store small manuals and instructions that you reference often, such as the instructions for sharpening your knives or the timing chart for your steamer or rice cooker.

You can see my own recipe binder on your video tutorials page at *clutterdiet.com/homeofficevideos*.

**Obviously by now you can probably tell that I like Evernote, and I have started using Evernote for all of my new recipes that I try.** I am finding them online or taking snapshots of them from books or magazines, and then tagging them "Dinners" or "Breakfasts" or "Soups" or any combination of tags that make sense. After I try the recipe, I then either tag it as a "Keeper" and write additional notes in it about what we liked, or I delete it if it wasn't good. I am cooking with my iPad in the kitchen to follow the recipes.

**Pinterest is a great place to find new recipes, probably too many!** Start a board for various types of recipes you like, pin them, and look to them for ideas when you are planning menus. If you want to use them and keep them, copy and paste them into Evernote or a word processing document, or print them and put them into your binder after you know they are good.

## Coupons

**Coupons can definitely save people lots of money, but they take time to manage. If you enjoy the process, by all means, please continue!** But many people have expressed guilt because they are not clipping and using all of the coupons that might be available to them.

So many families are eating fast food and unhealthy convenience meals because they can't seem to get it together to cook proper meals given all of their activities and demands. **I believe any family who is together enough to get a proper meal planned and put on the table gets huge credit for effort!** And if you are able to do that but are not checking your meal planning against the coupons you might have or what is in the weekly grocery circulars, I think you get a pass.

**I just want to give permission to all of the families out there who are doing the best they can to get a hot dinner ready to not feel bad because they have not done a perfect job of pulling together the coupons too.**

That said, if you want to clip and use coupons, **a standard "check file" accordion wallet available at any office supply store is more than adequate for organizing a normal volume of coupons.**

**Suggested categories for your coupon file:** Auto Services, Clothing, Electronics, Entertainment, Freq. Buyer Cards, Gift Cert., Groceries, Household, Lawn & Garden, Other, Personal Services, Pets, Restaurants, Unsorted.

You can place any new piles of coupons into Unsorted until you've had a chance to put them into the right section of the file.

**There are coupon file products for sale that have the categories pre-printed as well,** so you can search online or at your local discount store for those if you wish. Some of them have been engineered to snap onto your shopping cart and have some very clever designs.

If you want to start clipping coupons and being more deliberate about the savings, fit this habit into your Sunday Planning time, since you'll be planning menus and making your grocery list.

## Grocery Lists

Grocery shopping lists are best posted somewhere handy that all of the family can access and contribute to as they notice a need. The refrigerator door is a common place, or a bulletin board in the kitchen. **Make sure there is a pen there to mark things down, and to make shopping a little easier when you get to the store, I invented something I call the Quadrant Method.**

| Produce | Dry |
|---------|-----|
| avocados | cake mix |
| tomatoes | cinnamon |
| salad greens | kidney beans |
| cucumbers | lentils |
| | cornmeal |
| **Cold** | **Other** |
| milk | dental floss |
| eggs | alum. foil |
| orange juice | deodorant |
| deli turkey slices | birthday candles |

Each time you start a new list, **divide your sheet of paper into fourths with two lines**, as shown in this illustration.

**Label each quadrant:**
- Produce
- Dry (pantry items)
- Cold (freezer, deli, or dairy)
- Other (toiletries, pet needs, or cleaning supplies)

Anyone in the family can simply write a new item into the correct section. You save steps and hassle by knowing exactly what you need in each general area of the store.

I don't like using chalkboards or whiteboards for shopping lists, since they are not able to be carried along to the store with you. **However, if you like having a whiteboard, you can take a photo of your list and have it with you on your phone-- smart and easy!**

**I now prefer a combination of having an "old school" Quadrant paper list posted in our kitchen and using a smartphone app.** We mostly use the smartphone app, and the paper list is there for the family to use if they are not able to enter it into the app.

I like *Grocery IQ,* which is available for iPhone, iPad, and Android, and it's synchronized with its own web application. Other apps are also quite good, including Cozi.com (which has an amazing array of other great tools!) and OurGroceries.

Regardless of your choice of app, most of them share these features which are true of Grocery IQ. Here are some of the advantages of using an app:

- ✓ **Your phone is usually everywhere you are,** so you can add to your list at the odd random times something pops into your head.
- ✓ **Most of these apps are free.**
- ✓ **Lists are shared and synchronized**, so you and your significant other can always have the latest list wherever and whenever you need it. With some apps, you can even split up in the store and work off the same list in real-time! If my spouse checks off something on his iPhone over in the Produce section, I can see that he has picked up the item right then on my Android as I stand in Frozen Foods.
- ✓ **Easily add new items** by typing just a few letters.
- ✓ **Describe exactly what you want to avoid mistakes and returns.** (Decaf, sugar-free, lemon-flavored, etc.) Some apps also include a photo of the product packaging next to the item.
- ✓ **Scan almost any product's barcode with the app and instantly get its information in your list.** You can scan things in as you use them up in the kitchen.
- ✓ **Organize items into different lists by store,** so you can manage your Target or Walmart list right along with your grocery and warehouse store lists.
- ✓ **Minimize backtracking in the store,** because your list is automatically organized by aisle or section.
- ✓ **Jog your memory about what you frequently purchase by building a Favorites list,** so that you can quickly look over it for items you may have forgotten.
- ✓ **Email or text the list to almost anyone**, even if he or she doesn't have a smartphone.
- ✓ **Click the microphone button and speak your items into your list.** You say each item one at a time and wait for the search results, then click to verify your choice.

Now you've got your family's meals, school papers, and activities all figured out! Next we're going to tackle the huge paper monster of READING MATERIAL.

# READING MATERIAL

The availability of information is a great thing. However, **the expectations we put upon ourselves to digest this information can be unrealistic and stressful to the point of gluttonous excess.**

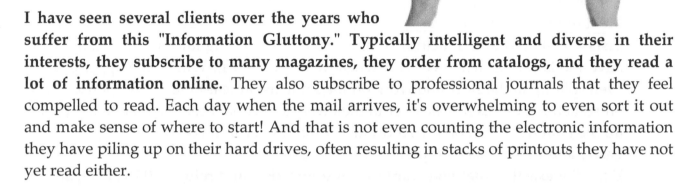

**I have seen several clients over the years who suffer from this "Information Gluttony." Typically intelligent and diverse in their interests, they subscribe to many magazines, they order from catalogs, and they read a lot of information online.** They also subscribe to professional journals that they feel compelled to read. Each day when the mail arrives, it's overwhelming to even sort it out and make sense of where to start! And that is not even counting the electronic information they have piling up on their hard drives, often resulting in stacks of printouts they have not yet read either.

**The compounding problem is that, even with the tremendous guilt and anxiety they feel as they survey the stacks around them, they continue to buy more and add more to the piles.**

## *Information Gluttony Strategies*

- ☑ **Accept the fact that you cannot ever possibly digest it all.** Just as you can only comfortably eat until you're full, there is only so much information one can consume before you run out of time and capacity.
- ☑ **Prioritize what your top three areas of focus are for learning at this time.** For one doctor client of mine, it was her practiced medical specialty, her culinary hobby, and her religious study. All other subjects were then considered second-tier. Re-evaluate this as your interests change.
- ☑ **Prevent more information from coming in.** Stop buying and subscribing to new things until you feel you're back in control. Unsubscribe to magazines you have not read and anything that does not contribute to learning in your three prioritized

subject areas. Make sure you check privacy policies when purchasing from catalogs or online stores so that you can prevent being added to more mailing lists. You can also manage catalog subscriptions at *www.catalogchoice.org*.

✓ **Purge all information older than a certain cutoff date that you determine.** For some, anything older than 3 months will be too old, and for others, anything older than 6 months or one year. Adjust this threshold to your comfort level, and then stick to it. Recycle your way back to a manageable stack or two.

✓ **Prune the information that continues to come in by continuing to unsubscribe to unread items and using a "limiting container" to keep the piles managed.** When the container, like a basket, is full, it's time to clean it out.

✓ **Stop feeling overly responsible for information.** Your house is NOT a library. You are NOT responsible for keeping everything for future reference, nor is it even possible. How could you ever find anything specific anyway if it's not indexed, and are you planning on doing that indexing? And what is better for indexing than the Internet? So there you go. Just Google it.

✓ **Go digital as much as possible.** Use RSS readers to aggregate blogs and other website feeds, so that you avoid printing out articles. And utilize Kindles, iPads, or other tablets instead of buying more physical books.

✓ **Take speed reading classes.** For better adult learning skills, I recommend my friend Abby Marks Beale's site, *RevItUpReading.com*.

✓ **If possible, get someone to pre-read for you.** Is there someone who understands you and your business well enough to skim through your professional publications and flag articles that will pertain to your needs?

**You can also prioritize your reading material by using our A-B-C-D method:**

✓ "A" magazines are ones you never want to miss or you must read for work.

✓ "B" publications are favorites but are not quite as important as the "A" ones.

✓ "C" publications are ones you are rarely reading, and

✓ "D" publications are ones you are not reading at all.

Most people have time to read only A and B items, so seriously consider getting rid of anything that is C or D.

**And what about that elusive "someday" when you're going to have extra time on your hands to catch up on your reading?** Sorry, but I really don't believe that "someday" is never going to come, especially when more new stuff keeps coming every day.

**Let's just accept this fact right now: No matter what your area of interest or industry, there is more information out there about it than you could ever possibly digest in your lifetime.** Consider blogs, websites, magazines, videos, newspaper articles, and even tweets. It's staggering.

**Accepting this fact is crucial** if you are ever going to reduce the number of books, newsletters, printouts and magazines in your physical environment (and electronic documents and bookmarks in your digital environment). And accepting this fact is also crucial if you're going to reduce the time you spend attempting to consume and manage all of this information.

**Instead of thinking of information as a giant all-you-can-eat buffet, think of it as a room service menu that you can order exactly what you want from as you need it.** Breathe for a second. The information is all there. You can search for it and find it when you want it, either online or in an actual library.

## Magazine Collections

**One of the most humorous things I notice in my work as a Professional Organizer is how many people collect** *National Geographic* **magazines.** I think of them as the "Golden Shelves of Glory" when I walk into a room and see them. Here's a photo of some in a basement, but often they are very prominently displayed in living rooms or in office shelving units.

**Funny thing—I have never met anyone who actually references them or does anything useful with them beyond**

**occasionally letting their kids cut them up for social studies projects.** (Clearly now that I have said this, I will hear from someone about how saving these won them a science project award, made them some money, saved someone's life, stopped a bullet, etc.)

**In my opinion, saving** *National Geographic,* **along with its close cousins** *The New Yorker* **and** *Architectural Digest,* **provides us examples of these three phenomena:**

- ☑ **"Perfectly Good" Syndrome.**

  "These are too nice to throw away... surely these have some kind of value! I don't want to waste them!" National Geographic's own website says that issues from the 1920s to the present are fairly easy to find. Are some of yours older than 1920? If so, they may be worth something to a serious collector (National Geographic's website lists these collectors). But if you have the typical last few decades' worth, they are a dime a dozen.

- ☑ **"Manifest Destiny/Collect Them All" Syndrome.**

  "I've collected these since I was a kid." So you keep on doing it, just because... but why? Really, why? This may have become an unconscious action, and you have a choice to stop doing it at any moment. Having a "complete" collection of these magazines doesn't provide any more value to your life than not having it. You can just stop.

- ☑ **"I'm a Sophisticated Person" Syndrome.**

  You're not even reading them when they arrive, but you're saving them because somewhere in your mind it makes you feel like you're the kind of person who *does* read them. Subscribing and saving them makes you absorb their knowledge by osmosis alone. And when people come over and look at your bookshelves, they know you're a literary, worldly kind of guy. Sometimes owning certain objects allows us to believe things about our own identity—things that might not reflect reality but instead reflect our aspirations and visions of our ideal selves.

**Questions for the Serious Collector:**

- ☑ **Do you ever refer to them?** How often?

- ☑ **Are they useful in any way?**

☑ **Are they beautiful?** Yes, they are Golden Shelves of Glory, but what else could be in their place that you might enjoy more, like favorite books or photos or artwork?

☑ **Have they added any value to your life,** enough to merit the space they occupy?

☑ **Have you indexed your collection?** In other words, if you needed information on Burkina Faso, would you know which issue to grab?

☑ **Could you find that same information online or in your public library**, without having to be "the keeper of the archives" yourself?

☑ **What would happen if you moved?** Do you realize how much your collection weighs and how much it would cost you to move it?

☑ **Do you realize that your kids do not want to have this collection?** (I am a betting kind of gal and I would take that bet.)

☑ **What is the cost of keeping it?** Storage costs money, particularly if you have offsite storage units. Golden Shelves of Glory represent many linear feet of shelf space that could be used for other more useful and relevant things.

**If you must keep some magazines... once again, our "Limiting Container" principle works beautifully.** Purchase enough magazine holders at an office supply store to hold your quota of them, say a year's worth. And that's it. Anything that won't fit into those magazine holders has to go.

**You can also practice the "One-In, One-Out" rule with magazines.** When a new magazine comes in, an old one gets recycled.

# FINANCIAL

Money matters, especially in your home office! So much of your activity in this space is either directly or indirectly related to finances, business or personal or both. Here's what you need to know:

## *Paying Bills*

☑ **Have a designated home for bill-paying supplies** like checks, deposit slips, letter openers, pens, payment coupon booklets, postage stamps, envelopes, return address labels, a calculator, and a stapler.

☑ **Decide on certain days to pay the bills, then stick to your plan consistently**. You might choose the 1st & 15th, 10th & 25th, every week, or every other week on a certain day. I pay my bills every Tuesday, and it gives me great peace of mind. (Our Clutter Diet members can use our customized e-mail reminder system to help them remember.)

☑ **Keep all bills together in one place as they arrive.** You can use a tray or vertical sorter to keep them visible and ready, or even a clothespin. Separating business bills from personal bills is a good strategy, or if you have multiple bank accounts, you can even separate bills based on which account will pay them.

☑ **Automate as much as possible, directly with your vendors.** You can set up payments with most vendors to pay automatically either by credit card or automatic draft.

☑ **Don't hand-write checks and mail them out if you don't have to!** Use your bank's online bill pay features for vendors who don't have automated payment options (or if you just prefer having more control). You can set up recurring payments that you never have to worry about again, like the mortgage payment, the orthodontist, or anything.

✓ **Simplify your number of bills by consolidating down to only 1-2 major credit cards** instead of multiple department store and gasoline cards. Try to get one that gives points for your favorite frequent flyer program, or cash back.

✓ **Pre-inked rubber stamps are fantastic.** Your return address on a rubber stamp is a big time-saver, and you can also get one made for endorsing checks for deposit with your name, "For Deposit Only" and your bank information on it. Also get a PAID stamp with rotating date wheels so you can breeze through notations on your bills quickly.

✓ **Go paperless.** Most major institutions would now prefer to send paperless bills, and it means less paper clutter for you to handle and file. Look on the envelope flap of your bill's return envelope or in the text of the bill itself to find out how your statements can be electronically received. Do make sure you have a good backup system on your hard drive, and be mindful that you no longer will have a physical reminder of the bill that needs payment. Make sure you have another Cue set up to remind you to pay the bill, since the actual paper won't be sitting in your stack.

✓ **Get complete freedom from all bills.** If you travel often, if you are paying bills for an elderly relative, or if you just don't like dealing with bills at all, you might like Paytrust.com. They are now owned by Intuit, and have been around for at least ten years. We used Paytrust when we went on a sabbatical in 2000. They assist you in changing all of your bills' addresses to their clearinghouse, where they receive them and scan all the bills in color. They notify you via e-mail that the bill has arrived and tell you what is going to happen next. You set up payment rules for each payee to automatically pay when the bill is received. You can set up rules like, "Pay this bill automatically within (x) days of receipt, as long as it's under (x) dollars." You can also use multiple bank accounts. Paytrust charges $9.95 per month.

## Keeping Paid Bills

Businesses need to document everything that is spent, so in general we recommend businesses keep every paid bill and receipt. But for household bills, depending upon your situation, you don't necessarily need to keep the statements and invoices that are already paid.

**One option for households is to keep a folder for paid bills and follow the "One-In-One-Out" rule.** When this month's is paid, put it in the folder and remove last month's to shred it, now that you know that there has not been a problem with the payment.

**Scanning is definitely another fine option,** and if you use Paytrust's service as described above, your bills will all be scanned and saved automatically (you never even get the paper sent to you). Services like *Shoeboxed.com* will scan paid bills and receipts for you at a very reasonable cost.

**Our favorite way to file paid bills, receipts, and bank statements is by month.** You can buy a brown accordion file in the office supply store marked January-December. Just put everything for each month in there, tie it up with a big bow at the end of the year and start over. You can keep these in archived storage for the 7-year period that is normally recommended (check with your accountant or attorney for retention advice specific to your situation, and see our section on Paper Retention Guidelines).

# Receipts

Businesses should keep all purchase receipts and should definitely use financial management software like QuickBooks to track and report on the information.

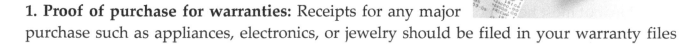

**In the case of your personal household transactions, however, many are routine and irrelevant, and keeping all receipts would be a waste of time and energy.** Do you really need a receipt to prove that you bought some gum?

**There are essentially 6 reasons that people should keep purchase receipts:**

**1. Proof of purchase for warranties:** Receipts for any major purchase such as appliances, electronics, or jewelry should be filed in your warranty files and retained as long as you own the item. We usually make files with the major heading "Warranties & Instructions" and then have folders for subcategories of Major Appliances, Small Appliances, Electronics, Computers & Peripherals, etc. depending on the person's buying habits.

**2. Proof of major expenses:** Receipts for any major expense for your car should be kept in a file for that vehicle, as long as you own it. Major home improvement expenses should be kept in a file for "Home Improvements & Repairs" and then kept with your tax records after you have sold the home.

**3. Merchandise returns or exchanges:** If you possibly could return an item (or if you gave it as a gift), you may want to hold onto the receipt for 30 days or as long as the store's return policy applies (some are only 14 days). After that point, you could either throw away the receipts or file them if you need them for warranty reasons. We recommend having a spot for these kinds of pending receipts, such as a slot in a letter sorter or a "waiting" folder, and cleaning it out periodically when full.

**4. Expense reimbursements:** You may need to be reimbursed for work expenses made with personal funds. First, find out if your company can give you a credit card to use for these items in the future to keep things simpler. You also might enjoy using NeatReceipts or NeatDesk, a scanner/software combination made just for this purpose.

**5. Budgeting and reconciling:** You may be trying to make sense of how much you spend in certain categories. With online banking providing more and more data, do you really need to track everything? If you feel you must keep receipts for this reason, we recommend having a simple January-December expandable accordion file to quickly and easily put them away.

**6. Tax deductions:** If you are going to tell the IRS something, you need to be ready to back it up. We recommend having an income tax file for each year. Always have at least one year's tax folder made up in advance so you'll be ready when the paper arrives. When you do have a receipt that will be tax deductible, you can jot a quick note on it first and then drop it in your tax file. Tax organization needs can vary widely depending on your situation, but most households don't have that much and one folder will do.

Again, please check with your attorney and/or accountant to verify what receipts you need to keep, but in general, the above rules apply to most personal household situations. If in doubt, an easy solution is sending all of your receipts to Shoeboxed.com for scanning, so then there are no decisions to be made and it's just done.

## Quicken Guilt

I have coined this phrase, "Quicken Guilt," to describe the situation we often see in home offices... We routinely ask a lot of assessment questions in our work as organizers, and one of them is whether they use any financial software. **People frequently get a sheepish look on their faces and say they know they "should" be using Quicken or some other financial software to track their spending, but they just aren't doing it.**

**People are often surprised when I say it's okay not to use financial software.** Most people, I am guessing 80-90% of our clients, do not reconcile their bank statements either. As long as you have some kind of check and balance on your spending, it's not necessary or realistic to enter in (or even download) every receipt you have and every penny you spend in your personal life.

Obviously, it's ideal to use Quicken and I really love their software in general, but it takes a lot of commitment to use it consistently the way it's intended. (I am talking about personal finances here, not business. We feel it's imperative to use QuickBooks or other financial software diligently for any business.)

**Online banking has made it more realistic for people to keep tabs on their accounts.** We recommend if you are not going to reconcile and use Quicken, you at least need to regularly log in and review your transactions to make sure identity theft does not occur (see next section!). We also think it's a good idea to make a "snapshot" spreadsheet periodically to look at balances on all accounts and check in with your situation. I am sure not everyone agrees with me on this one... but I know that I have many colleagues in my industry who do.

*(As with anything else in this book, please check with your own attorney or accountant to advise you officially on financial and legal matters.)*

If you are using Quicken or QuickBooks for your business, create an Action tray or basket for anything that needs to be entered, and designate a time when you will do this entry, either once a week or once a month, just like you designate a time to pay bills. If you can delegate this data entry, even better!

## *Avoid Identity Theft*

A couple of times in the last few years, I have had my debit or credit card number stolen. This last time, someone used our business checking card to buy $160+ worth of pet supplies, with the billing address as *mine* and the shipping address as some lady in Utah. But I caught it! HA! Too bad for you, Dishonest Utah Pet Lady!

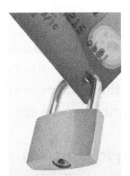

**How did I catch it? By simply reviewing my statements.** An easy habit that takes almost no time, but can save you hundreds or even thousands of dollars! I would never have known if I hadn't looked, because the card was still in my wallet.

When I saw the charge for pet supplies, I called our bank, the charge was reported, I was refunded for the amount, my card was cancelled, and a new one was on the way. It took about 15 minutes.

An interview with a notorious identity thief said that this is how they often get away with credit card fraud... **they charge something and wait to see if you notice, and if you don't, they ring up the charges until your card is maxed out.**

Organizing really helps keep you safe from a lot of identity theft issues, at least making you able to catch them before they get worse.

**Here are four proactive habits you can cultivate which take very little time to do:**

> **1. Shred**. Get yourself a good shredder and shred anything you're discarding that might compromise your identity, your finances, your privacy, or your reputation. See our video tutorials page at *clutterdiet.com/homeofficevideos* for tips on buying a shredder.

**2. Process mail regularly.** The longer mail stays in piles, the longer a thief has to get away with something you didn't catch. And the longer it sits there, the bigger the piles get, and the less likely you will actually look at the statements after you open them. See our chapter on Processing Information.

**3. Review your statements regularly.** I recommend organizing your finances by having one day a week as an office day to pay bills and get administrative tasks checked off. While you are logged into your bank accounts, you can easily skim through the recent charges to make sure they look right. It takes maybe 30 seconds to a minute to review a week's worth of transactions.

**4. Review credit reports annually (at least).** The government sanctioned website for credit reports is *www.annualcreditreport.com*, where you are entitled to a free report each year from each of the three major credit reporting agencies. Reading these over will quickly show you whether someone's opening strange new accounts under your name, and if there are other errors, you can fix them and keep your credit sparkling clean.

According to statistics, out of every 100 of you reading this, seven of you will definitely experience identity theft this year. **So remember, MAIL PILES MAKE THIEVES SMILE!** Stay on top of your paper piles and bills.

**Aside from these habits related to organizing, here are a few more good practices to help prevent identity theft:**

- ✓ **Mail things from a secure location.** Avoid putting checks outside in the outgoing mail where they are vulnerable.
- ✓ **Clone your wallet once a year**—make a photocopy of everything, front and back. January is a great time to do this, and we remind our Clutter Diet members every year at the right time. If your wallet is stolen, you'll have a reminder of everything you were carrying, as well as all of the relevant numbers and notification hotlines.
- ✓ **Keep important identity documents hidden safely away in your home**. You don't want to leave a passport or social security card out where an untrustworthy person working inside your home could gain access to it.

✓ **Use secure passwords.** Our section on passwords in the Electronic Information chapter which has more about how to store them safely.

✓ **Be careful what you click.** Do not provide payment or identity information to any site that does not have SSL encryption (padlock symbol on your browser and an "S" at the end of https://). If you are in any doubt as to whether an email is legitimately from your bank, from Facebook, from Paypal, or from the Better Business Bureau, DON'T click any of the links or open any attachments!

## Taxes

**As stated already, if you are running a business, you definitely need to account for every receipt and all of your accounting should be in order.** QuickBooks is a very powerful tool that can grow with you as your business grows, and everything can be entered there and filed away.

Doing your taxes for your business is relatively simple if you keep up with your financial entry throughout the year. **If you use a bookkeeping service or accountant for your taxes, they can do almost everything from your QuickBooks file alone. I highly recommend utilizing tax professionals for your business, as they save you money and time, and they can offer valuable perspectives on your business.**

Your personal taxes can be much simpler, since most people don't need to keep every receipt and account for every penny. **Mainly you need to understand which papers you need to collect to complete your tax return.**

This checklist tool from H&R Block at *http://bit.ly/taxeschecklist* is an easy way to figure out what to save and separate out for tax season. **For most households, setting up one folder for "Income Tax- Current Year" will be adequate for collecting these documents.**

**Documenting your donations of household goods and clothing is one small new habit can save you hundreds of dollars on your personal taxes.** When you donate to Goodwill®, use our Donate for Dollars tracking sheet (on the left side of our page at *clutterdiet.com/freetips*) to list what you're giving away, and then use ItsDeductible.com or

CharityDeductions.com to ascertain the fair market value of those donations. **Many people save literally hundreds of dollars investing just a few minutes on these sites!**

**How long should you keep your tax records?** See our section on Paper Retention Guidelines in our Paper Reference chapter.

Each year when you do your tax return, it's a great time to purge your files from the years past. See our section on *Arms' Length Reference: Archiving Older Files* in our Paper Reference chapter.

# WORKSPACE

To tackle the physical space of your home office, you'll need a few tools and supplies, and you'll need to have a general approach for the project along with some specific advice for certain areas. This chapter includes all of this, along with a thorough checklist of "The Well-Equipped Office," a diagram of what an office might look like with these systems in place, and advice on how to share your space with others.

## *Your Organizing Toolkit*

☑ **Heavy-duty trash bags, lawn and leaf size:** Organizing tends to generate heavy duty trash, and you will need heavy-duty bags. Anything less than 1.1 mil of thickness, which you can read on the package's fine print, will lead to heartache and mess. I personally prefer drawstring closure ties as well.

☑ **Trash can:** Make sure it's large enough to handle a lot of trash. Otherwise it will get full too quickly, and you will get frustrated.

☑ **Recycling bin:** Bring the large bin in from the garage, or use paper grocery sacks or other alternative containers.

☑ **Shredder:** A good quality shredder is essential for any home office. See our special section on shredding for more information.

**Optional Additions:**

- **Goo-Gone**, for removing stickers
- **Museum Putty**, for securing items on shelves and keeping drawer dividers from sliding
- **Sticky notes**, various sizes
- **Furniture marking pens,** for touching up furniture scratches
- **Cable ties,** for cinching up cords and cables
- **Paper towels/cleaning rags**

Museum Putty, a 3-ft. measuring tape, and a timer are all available in our online store for your convenience. (*clutterdiet.com/products*)

- ✓ **Label maker:** You need only a handheld label maker, such as those by Brother or Dymo, and there is no reason to buy the more expensive console-style devices. Our preference is for QWERTY style keyboards for a more intuitive typing experience.

- ✓ **Paper grocery bags and/or boxes for sorting**: Paper sacks are perfect for sorting because you can write on them, they stand up on their own, they are pretty tough, and you can just give them away if they are filled with donation items. Boxes are also good, but they are bulkier to store.

- ✓ **"Elsewhere" Box:** Use one of your paper bags or boxes for this purpose... we'll explain more later.

- ✓ **Permanent markers:** We prefer Sharpie® Retractables.

- ✓ **Timer:** Use a timer to remind you if you want to stop working at a certain time, and timers are also great tools for overcoming procrastination. Bargain with yourself to do something for only ten or 15 minutes. Once you get started, you may even want to continue for a longer time.

- ✓ **Measuring tape:** A large measuring tape is great for so many reasons. Measure shelves and other items before you go shopping for containers. You also might need to measure furniture before deciding to move it. We recommend having a small three-foot measuring tape in your purse or on your keychain for use while shopping. (I love having one of these keychain tapes so much that we had some of our own made to sell in our online store.)

- ✓ **Scissors or a box knife:** You'll need something sharp for cutting open packages, removing price tags, and opening boxes.

- ✓ **Paper and pen for notes:** You'll probably have a shopping list going of things you need to buy to complete your work, and you'll need to jot down the measurements for certain shelves, items, or cabinet.

---

☑ **Calendar and task list:** The basic Commitment tools you decided back in our section on Choice Management. You'll need these for noting tasks and scheduling actions and appointments.

☑ **Water or other beverage:** Go ahead and get something to drink so you won't get distracted by that later. Preferably use a container with a cap on it, so it won't spill on things amid the clutter.

☑ **Phone(s):** Grab your cordless phone and/or your mobile phone so that you don't have to scramble when they ring! Alternatively, you can just turn them off to avoid the distraction. If you do answer the phone, make sure you don't get sidetracked with your conversation. You may be able to keep sorting while you talk, depending upon the type of call and what you're sorting.

## The O.R.D.E.R. Approach for Organizing Anything

**Many unsuccessful organizing projects have been started by "diving in" without thinking through the space.** Our SpaceScaping® O.R.D.E.R. acronym provides the correct approach for almost any organizing project, whether it's a filing system, a closet, a chemistry lab or a garage. My team and I have used this approach for every project we have taken on with our clients, and now you can apply it to your workspace.

**Strategizing is crucial to the success of your project! You _must_ outline the plan first.** Sometimes this planning requires objectivity, and you may have lost yours. You have probably been looking at the space too long. You have been living in it and contributing to its current state, and the contents have begun to look like "wallpaper" to you—just part of the scenery.

**To gain the objectivity you need on your project,**

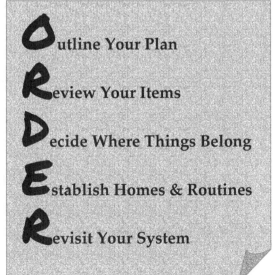

**O**utline Your Plan

**R**eview Your Items

**D**ecide Where Things Belong

**E**stablish Homes & Routines

**R**evisit Your System

**I recommend taking photographs of the space.** Somehow that gives you a new perspective on a room. From a photograph you may realize things you don't notice when you're in the space in person, and it also gives you a "Before" photo you may be very proud to have later!

**For additional objectivity, have a friend visit the space and help you go over the questions in the Outline Your Plan section below.** Essentially you need someone who doesn't live in the space with you to give you a fresh pair of eyes.

## Outline Your Plan

**The first question I always ask is, "Who is using this space?"** This may seem obvious to you, but think through it anyway. There may be factors you have not considered regarding children, housekeepers or guests.

Next look at the four "F's" of your room (yes, we have four "F" words!): Features, Function, Flow and Frequency.

### FEATURES:

What is the skeleton of the room? Which features are changeable and which are not? Notice the furniture, plumbing, walls, closets and doors. Think about everything differently…what if you removed a door and left a closet open? What if you had a different piece of furniture?

### FUNCTION:

**What functions are happening in this space?** Think about the functions you would like to happen here, such as exercising or studying, that you might want to add once the space is improved.

**One of the pitfalls of a home office is that often people are trying to provide too many functions in too little space, usually trying to meet all of their wants and needs in one spare bedroom.** We've seen home offices also attempting to accommodate crafts, sewing, guests, scrapbooking, reading, meditating, exercising, and kids' playspace.

Trying to take any three (or more) of these and making them operate in one small room is extremely difficult, and **I recommend focusing on two main functions at the most.**

Room dividers like screens and shelving units can sometimes be effective at separating the space, but typically only if there are two major functions occurring and the room is not too small. **You may need to move the excess functions to other rooms, or even give up the idea of that activity being in your home.** We've seen clients who have downsized in a move, sold their treadmill or other exercise equipment and started going to a gym instead.

## FLOW:

**How do these features and functions relate to each other? Are there any obvious patterns here? Are there any "logjams" where clutter seems to be aggregating? Why?**

You might notice the "chain of custody" of the items—where did they come from? Can you stop the inflow of new items in some way? If you can't stop it, can you create a better system to accommodate it?

## FREQUENCY:

**How often do these functions occur and how important are they?** If you exercise three times a week, the treadmill has earned its position in the room. If you exercise once or twice a year on that treadmill and otherwise use it as a place to pile books and papers, it probably needs to go. (Do consider "workwalking," though-- I have written a lot of this book while walking on my treadmill! I have a guide to workwalking on my blog at *http://bit.ly/workwalking*, and I own a super nifty treadmill desk that you can see in this YouTube video at *http://bit.ly/lorietrekdesk*.)

**Synthesize what you've learned to make a plan for your room. Think of it as a puzzle you are solving.** Each function should fit into its own zone and all of the functions should flow together.

**Don't worry if you don't know what to do exactly! Here's a secret: I often don't.** Sometimes it takes wading into the project to create the best solutions. But having done your homework, with these functions all ascertained, you will feel the solution is rather obvious when it appears.

**Our last question is, "Are there any obvious supplies needed?"** Now this is where people can get in trouble. One of the biggest mistakes we see is people going out to buy all kinds of organizing supplies before they know what they need.

You can intelligently determine some items, however, that will most certainly be required. Our Well-Equipped Office section in this chapter will be very useful to think though this—during this stage of the process, make sure you go over that information. You may realize you really need some shelving or a desk or some file folders. If you are really sure, you can measure carefully and purchase the supplies needed to get started.

**O**utline Your Plan

**R**eview Your Items

**D**ecide Where Things Belong

**E**stablish Homes & Routines

**R**evisit Your System

## Review Your Items

Now that you have a plan, you need to review the items that currently live there. Where within the room do you start? Here are a few strategies:

-  **Circular:** Pick a spot near the door and sort thoroughly in a circular pattern around the room until you return to that spot.
- **Outside-In:** Start with flat surfaces like tables and desks, then move to piles on the floor, then tackle whatever is inside drawers and cabinets.
- **Centralized:** Centralize everything first before sorting. You can clear everything out of the room that doesn't belong, leaving only the furniture, and take everything into a larger "staging area" space to sort through it, like a big dining table.

In this stage you are sorting things into categories based on what makes sense. Office supplies go together, printer supplies and paper go together, knickknacks and décor, and so on.

## REVIEWING CAUTION #1:

**We refer to the Reviewing stage as the "Scary Phase." Everything is spread out. Don't worry!** Visibility is crucial to the organizing process, and the only way to create this visibility and make better decisions about your stuff is to get it all out where you can see it and make your choices. It gets a little worse before it gets better, but just keep going.

## REVIEWING CAUTION #2:

**Your sorting session is meant to be fast and practical, not a work session for tasks or a trip down memory lane.** As we said back in the first chapter, your job is to focus on SORTING and SCHEDULING. Sort it out, and if it requires action, write it down on your task list or calendar and keep going. If you are tempted to sit and reminisce or to start "doing" some of the tasks you find, STOP and redirect yourself. This is where having a friend to help can really be useful.

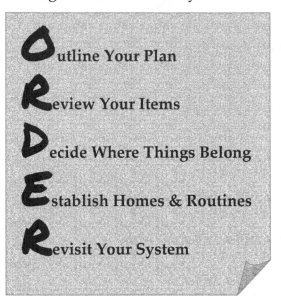

**O**utline Your Plan

**R**eview Your Items

**D**ecide Where Things Belong

**E**stablish Homes & Routines

**R**evisit Your System

## REVIEWING CAUTION #3:

**"Elsewhere" items often appear while sorting, such as items that need to be returned and items that belong in another room like the kitchen or bedroom.** Create a group of these Elsewhere items right where you are and keep going. Don't get distracted taking these things somewhere else and abandon your project. If there are many items, you can create subgroups based on where the items go to make putting them away easier later. Paper grocery sacks or shopping bags are useful for sorting these Elsewhere items.

## Decide Where Things Belong

Reviewing and sorting goes along concurrently with the next letter in our O.R.D.E.R. acronym, D for Decide. As you're sorting you'll be making decisions about your things.

**As I explained in the first chapter, when you really get down to the essence of our role as Professional Organizers,** *we help people make decisions.* It's that simple. The root cause of clutter is procrastination of these decisions, and we help you bring them to the forefront and bust through them. **Being more organized in your life means being more decisive—about your stuff, your time and your information.**

**One of the tools we use to help people make decisions is our A-B-C-D method of prioritization.** We refer to things as A, B, C or D in terms of their frequency of use, and we refer to places as A, B, C or D in terms of their accessibility.

| Things | Priorities | Places |
|---|---|---|
| Pens, stapler, phone, scissors | **A** <br> Used frequently, even daily. | Handiest drawer or on top of desk |
| 3-hole punch, paper cutter, staples, rubber stamps | **B** <br> Used often; weekly or monthly. | Above, below or behind "A" items, enclosed in cabinet or drawer |
| Holiday decorations, trade show signage, travel items | **C** <br> Used rarely or seasonally. | Higher shelves, less accessible places—even attic |
| Archived documents, filed receipts, tax records | **D** <br> Never or seldom used. | Completely out of daily flow- in least accessible location or offsite storage. |

**"A" things are used frequently, even daily or multiple times per day, like your favorite pens or your phone.** "A" spaces are your desktop, credenza, and other flat surfaces; the most eye-level, easy to reach shelves; the handiest drawers; and the other most easily accessible spaces.

**"B" things are used often but just not as frequently as the "A" things, like refills for office supplies, extra paper, or a 3-hole punch.** They need to be put in "B" spaces, meaning behind "A" things, above or below "A" things, inside a cabinet or in otherwise less accessible spots.

**"C" things are used, but they are used infrequently or seasonally, such as holiday decorations or trade show signs.** They need to be in "C" places that are less accessible and completely out of the way of the daily flow of your workspace.

**"D" things are items you actually do not use, but you feel you have to keep them anyway, like old tax records or former client files.** "D" things need to be in "D" places, as out of the way as possible. Of course, we encourage you to think carefully about discarding "D" things if legally possible, since by definition you are not using them.

People always joke with us that they have "E" and "F" things, but everything you own really does fit in this model somewhere. This A-B-C-D prioritizing tool is a useful way of thinking and talking about your stuff, it provides additional objectivity, and it quickly helps you decide how you're using something and where it should be. **The goal is to get the "A" things in the "A" places, and the "D" things in the "D" places.** We see all the time things that are "C" things in "A" places, and so on, taking up valuable real estate in your space.

During this phase of reviewing and deciding, it's helpful to ask yourself some questions when you are unsure about an item. Here are some of our favorites:

> ✓ **When is the last time you used this item?** If it's been more than a year, it's unlikely that you will use it again. (Make it two years if you must, but set a time frame and stick to it.) If you're not sure and can't make a decision, you can mark the item with a note indicating the date, and during a future project you can see how long it's been since you reviewed and decided upon it before. If you have lots of small items like these, bundle them together in one box and seal it up with the date on the outside.

- ☑ **What is a scenario in which you can actually see yourself using it, and how likely is that to happen?** Sometimes people say "I might need it someday," and we ask them this question. We've gotten some ridiculous and hilarious answers about far-fetched scenarios that are not going to happen! (Do take care to observe responsible retention guidelines for your information, however… see our section on this earlier in the Paper Reference chapter.)

- ☑ **What does it cost (in both time and money) to replace this item? And how hard would it be to find and purchase this item again?** Sometimes you haven't used something in a long time and are keeping it "just in case," when in reality it is easily replaced if you need it again. Is the item worth taking up your valuable "A" and "B" space if it's not really an "A" or "B" item in terms of frequency?

- ☑ **What is the worst case scenario if you did get rid of this item?** The answer to this question might not be so bad, and just the act of stopping to consider it makes things obvious.

**The bottom line is that you need to make room in your workspace for your "A" and "B" items and really think hard about anything else you don't use as often.**

During this Reviewing and Deciding phase, you begin to accumulate various piles, which you will deal with during the later phases of the project:

- ☑ **Keep:** Various categories of items you'll be saving and storing here
- ☑ **Elsewhere:** Items that belong elsewhere in your home or another place, as well as returns
- ☑ **Trash:** Garbage, recycling and shredding
- ☑ **Donations/Give to Friend:** Items you are giving to charity or others (find your nearest Goodwill® donation center at *http://locator.goodwill.org*)
- ☑ **Sell:** Items for consignment stores, Craigslist, eBay or a garage sale

## Establish Homes & Routines

Now that you've made decisions about your belongings and disposed of things you don't need, you can establish homes for them and routines for keeping the space maintained.

**Everything needs a home.** If you've decided something is worth keeping, it deserves an established place of its own. Finding things later depends upon this concept! I sometimes have fun asking audiences if they know where their underwear is located. Almost everyone does have a home for their underwear, typically a certain drawer (a drawer for your drawers!). And most people know exactly where the milk is in the refrigerator, because there is a spot for that. Let's translate this concept to the rest of the items in your home office, as much as possible.

One consideration for establishing a home for items is based on our A-B-C-D ideas, putting frequently used items in the most accessible spaces and so on.

**O**utline Your Plan

**R**eview Your Items

**D**ecide Where Things Belong

**E**stablish Homes & Routines

**R**evisit Your System

**Another consideration for establishing homes is the "point-of-use."** Put extra ink cartridges by the printer, for example. Where are you going to be when you need this item most? It's possible that duplicate items might be desirable when considering point-of-use. For example, you might have multiple pairs of scissors in your home for the office, the kitchen, and the gift wrapping supplies.

**Labeling helps tremendously in establishing the home for an item.** Here are a few favorite ways to label your stuff:

- ✓ **Sharpie® permanent markers.** We really like the retractable kind, because you don't have to fumble with a cap and potentially lose it, and it's a one-hand operation to click it open instead of a two-hand operation to pull the cap off. You can write directly on plastic and paper and almost anything else. We also love the metallic versions of these markers, as the silver ink shows up well on dark items. You can write directly onto a black videotape, for example (if you still have those around).
- ✓ **Label makers.** Affixing a printed label to your bins, shelves, and baskets is the best way to communicate the home for the items you're storing.
- ✓ **String tags.** When your label tape won't easily stick to the container's surface by itself, such as on a wicker basket, a round string tag is an attractive way to provide a

labeling surface. I like the Avery 11031 Metal Rim String Tags, the 1-9/16" size. If you care about the aesthetics of the project you're doing, string the tag with a colorful ribbon instead of the provided white cotton string.

☑ **Binder clips.** I invented this idea for labeling while in the shower one day thinking about a solution to a challenging problem for a client! Medium black binder clips are extremely inexpensive and are available at any office supply store. Try this solution: print a label on your label maker and adhere it to the back of the binder clip, then clip it onto any very narrow edge such as a tray. Fold the chrome parts back out of the way, or just squeeze sideways to remove them, leaving only the black portion of the clip there. Watch a video about how I use them on your video tutorials page at *clutterdiet.com/homeofficevideos*.

☑ **Printable label sheets and label printers.** If you have multiple labels to print at once, choose a label sheet to run through your printer and format the labels in your word processing software. You can also buy a special printer that prints rolls of labels to have always at the ready.

**Are you out of storage space?** Here are some tricks for finding more:

☑ **Go vertical.** Make sure you have maximized use of all your wall space and any wasted space between shelves. "Helper shelves" are accessories that provide one extra level of storage if you don't have adjustable shelving.

☑ **Don't forget the backs of doors.** Look up the word "overdoor" at sites like Organize.com or ContainerStore.com to see a large selection of products. Cabinet doors may also provide some storage options.

☑ **Go deep.** Make the most use of deep cabinets and corners by using turntables, also known as "Lazy Susans."

☑ **Hang from the ceiling.** If you want to move some of your "C" and "D" storage items out of your home office, overhead racks for the garage are a great option, with many brands on the market providing what they call the "second attic."

☑ **Get radical.** Rip out that closet that is not serving your needs. If you use a spare bedroom as an office, a closet configuration with hanging rods for a wardrobe is not the right solution. Add several rows of adjustable shelving there to provide proper storage for your supplies instead.

**Establishing routines is also part of this phase.** You've created the homes for these items, but there is a system involved in maintaining it. What are the specific steps required to keep this area in good shape?

In your home office, those maintenance tasks might look like this:

- Bring in the mail to be sorted
- Take out the full recycling bin to empty in the garage
- Empty the shredder
- Go through your reading basket when full
- File Handy Reference material in "To Be Filed" basket
- Process inbox weekly
- Etc…

Take note of these specific tasks, even if you just think through them in your mind without writing them down, because they are crucial to the success of your project over time.

## Revisit Your System

**The final step in our O.R.D.E.R. process is to Revisit the systems you've created. Few things are perfect the first time.** Most systems and spaces need a little tweaking here and there, particularly because life goes on and things do change. This process is referring to your physical workspace in particular, and as you consider your information processing, you'll be thinking through those as you "CORRECT" in those systems each week.

**O**utline Your Plan

**R**eview Your Items

**D**ecide Where Things Belong

**E**stablish Homes & Routines

**R**evisit Your System

Always look for how to make things easier and more obvious, and make the space reflect you and your style. After some time, look for the "logjams" of piled up clutter and go through asking yourself questions about them again.

You may find roadblocks like this one that are simple to solve, or you may have to deal with behavioral issues around maintaining the space. **Ask for help! I have put together some resources for you at the end of this book in the Get Help chapter.**

## The Well-Equipped Office

As you are Outlining your Plan for your workspace, here is an illustration of placement of many of the concepts we've discussed throughout this eBook. Your own office may be very different, but it may help you get the idea of how you could configure some of the basic elements of a successful home office.

If you'd like to print this diagram and these checklists separately with proper page breaks, go directly to a printable PDF version at *clutterdiet.com/officechecklist*.

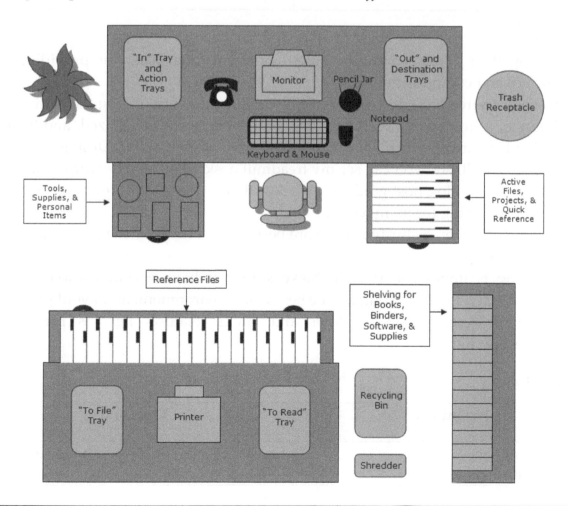

# The Well-Equipped Office Supplies List

## Furniture

| Essentials | Optional |
|---|---|
| ❑ Desk *(include storage drawers and file drawers)*<br>❑ Filing cabinet<br>❑ Cabinets and/or shelving for books, binders, software, and supplies<br>❑ Chair | ❑ Credenza or cart for printer, paper cutter, or other items that may detract from available surface area on your desk<br>❑ Table and chairs for collaborative meeting space<br>❑ Chair mat *(for rolling chair if necessary)* |

**Furniture Tips:**

- L-shaped or U-shaped desk configurations are often best for providing writing surface and computing surface.
- Consider a treadmill desk or a standing desk! Studies are finding that sitting for long hours of sedentary work is more dangerous than we ever realized, and being more active is relatively easy if you have the right equipment. TrekDesk is an option for any treadmill, and you can see my treadmill desk video at *http://bit.ly/lorietrekdesk* and read my blog post guide to "Workwalking" at *http://bit.ly/workwalking* that I have been doing for many years.
- Rolling chairs on a sturdy surface are best. Make sure your chair is comfortable and adjustable.
- Lighting is important as well. Make sure you have a combination of ambient, overhead, and task lighting for the best work environment, and avoid glare on your computer screen from windows and lamps. Natural light is preferred over fluorescent lighting.

## Accessories

| Essentials | Optional |
|---|---|
| ❑ "In" tray or basket<br>❑ "Out" tray or basket | ❑ Multiple paper trays for using as action or destination trays—can be used for: |

- ❑ "To File" tray or basket
- ❑ "To Read" tray or basket
- ❑ "Pencil Jar" to contain pens, pencils, highlighters, and scissors in the most accessible location
- ❑ Drawer dividers for tools and supplies inside drawers
- ❑ Recycling bin
- ❑ Trash receptacle

- o specific people
- o specific places
- o outgoing mail
- o calls
- o bills
- o data entry items
- ❑ Reading supplies in a small box or pouch inside the "To Read" basket
  - o blade for clipping pages
  - o small stapler with refill staples
  - o highlighter pens
  - o Post-It® flags & notes
  - o pen and pencil

## Computer Hardware & Software

| Essentials | Optional |
|---|---|
| ❑ Desktop Computer or Notebook<br>❑ Monitor(s) (A *New York Times* article said you get a 20-30% increase in productivity when you have two monitors!)<br>❑ Keyboard<br>❑ Mouse with scrolling wheel<br>❑ Printer<br>❑ Surge protector strip with adequate protection against electrical damage<br>❑ Established suite of office software, such as Microsoft Office® (*including time management, spreadsheet, and word processing applications*) | ❑ Additional software, such as financial, graphic design, desktop publishing, or database applications<br>❑ Wireless keyboard & mouse<br>❑ Writeable DVD drive<br>❑ Large computer screen to reduce eyestrain<br>❑ Battery backup unit<br>❑ External hard drive for data backups<br>❑ Router & receivers for wireless networking<br>❑ All-in-one printer/copier/scanner/fax (*All-in-one units can be detrimental if the printer is shared by active users whose needs may conflict.*)<br>❑ Copier |

| | |
|---|---|
| | ❑ Scanner |
| | ❑ Monitor riser-- keeps you more comfortable ergonomically, raises your webcam up to a better level, provides storage within and under (watch a video about this at *clutterdiet.com/homeofficevideos*) |

## Telephone Equipment

| Essentials | Optional |
|---|---|
| ❑ Telephone<br>❑ Voice messaging system<br>❑ Headset | ❑ Cordless phone<br>❑ Wireless headset<br>❑ Automatic receiver pickup device for wireless headset<br>❑ Speakerphone with mute button |

## Tools

| Essentials | Optional |
|---|---|
| ❑ Stapler<br>❑ Staple remover<br>❑ Tape dispenser<br>❑ Scissors<br>❑ Label maker (*Handheld type is all most people need, not the console/typewriter size.*)<br>❑ Hole punch<br>❑ Pencil sharpener<br>❑ Letter opener, preferably razor blade type instead of knife style<br>❑ Postage scale<br>❑ Ruler | ❑ 3-hole punch<br>❑ Paper cutter<br>❑ Automatic stapler<br>❑ Custom self-inking stamps for return addresses and check endorsements<br>❑ USB removable media drive ("keychain" or "thumb" drive)<br>❑ Bulletin board<br>❑ Small set of handyman tools, such as a screwdriver, hammer, and assorted hardware<br>❑ Lap desk for working away from your desk on your notebook computer |

- ❑ Calculator
- ❑ Clock *(You may need only the one on your computer screen.)*
- ❑ Shredder

## Consumable Supplies

| Essentials | | Optional |
|---|---|---|
| ❑ Staples<br>❑ Refill tape for tape dispenser<br>❑ Refill tape for your label maker<br>❑ Pens<br>❑ Pencils<br>❑ Highlighters<br>❑ Sharpie® permanent markers *(in various sizes- good for labeling)*<br>❑ Hanging file folders<br>❑ Extra file tabs or labels<br>❑ Binder clips, assorted sizes<br>❑ Paper clips<br>❑ Blank CDs or other writable media<br>❑ Scratch paper | ❑ Rubber bands<br>❑ Various sizes of mailing envelopes<br>❑ Packing tape<br>❑ Return address labels<br>❑ Post-It® Notes of various sizes<br>❑ Stamps<br>❑ Notepads of your choice *(legal pad, spiral)*<br>❑ Batteries of assorted sizes<br>❑ Ink refills for printer<br>❑ Paper for printer | ❑ 3-ring binders<br>❑ Sheet protectors<br>❑ Dividers for binders<br>❑ Label sheets for your printer in various sizes *(address, shipping, CDs, diskettes)*<br>❑ Telephone message pads<br>❑ Cardstock paper<br>❑ Key tags for labeling keys<br>❑ Laminating sheets<br>❑ Pushpins/thumbtacks<br>❑ Business stationery-- letterhead, envelopes, note cards, business cards<br>❑ Shredder oil/lubricating sheets |

## *Got a Lot to Shred?*

**Practice safe disposal! Shredding is more important than ever with identity theft being one of the fastest growing crimes.** We recommend that every household have a shredder, and that you purchase one that shreds a minimum thickness of eight sheets at a time, preferably more. Think about one envelope with two sheets of paper folded inside it—the two pages folded into thirds make six thicknesses of paper. If you count the two thicknesses of the envelope holding it, that is a total of eight sheets. If you've already identified that you want to shred something, you will want to be able to stick the envelope directly into the shredder without opening it.

**You should buy a name-brand shredder of high quality, as shredders tend to break easily.** Mark my words; you will be frustrated if you get a cheap shredder that clogs! It's an investment, like an insurance policy against crime. I like buying shredders that also have the ability to shred CDs and DVDs safely, since our electronic data is sensitive. Shredder blades do need to be oiled, and you can buy special shredder oil for this purpose, but instead I like the shredder lubricating sheets that you just feed through periodically. These sheets are much neater than their liquid counterpart and are simple to put through after you've just shredded a large batch of paper.

**What should you shred?** Err on the side of caution; in other words, it's better to shred too much than too little. Shred anything you are disposing that has financial information on it, account numbers, personal identification information or medical information. **We always say to shred anything that would damage your identity, your finances, your privacy or your reputation!**

**If you have a big backlog of shredding to do, such as multiple boxes full of old papers in your garage, a document management company in your hometown likely has a mobile shredding truck that can come to your home and do the shredding onsite.** My preference is for those trucks that grind up your paper in front of a camera mounted inside the truck itself, while you watch on the monitor they have. Watching this is actually quite interesting. Your paper gets chewed up into giant rotating Dudley-Do-Right villain blades.

You witness the shredding yourself and they give you a "Certificate of Destruction" right on the spot, which makes you feel secure about parting with the information.

Clearly a mobile shredding truck is the most secure and convenient way to handle your confidential documents, but if that is not available in your area or your street is not accessible to the truck, there are other ways to get it done. **The second most secure way is to bring the papers yourself to a shredding company's location and observe the destruction there.** If you want a convenient option and are not as worried about witnessing the destruction, the shredding companies will typically be able to send a truck to pick up your documents and securely transport them to their location to destroy them.

**Ask the shredding company if there are restrictions on what they will accept.** The shredding trucks we use will even grind up old floppy disks and CDs, and it's okay to put hanging folders through with the metal braces in them. But your shredder may have a different policy regarding these items, so ask if you are not sure.

**Keep your ears open for a free community shredding event in your area.** Shredding companies commonly will provide a "drive-through" shredding experience once or twice a year as part of a bigger citywide promotion of some kind, like Earth Day, for example. Usually they have a limit on how many boxes or pounds they will accept per household, so do check this detail before driving your boxes over there.

## Velcro®, the Magic Organizing Tool!

Velcro hook and loop fastening strips are so useful for organizing your workspace that they merit having their own section in this chapter!

Here are some tips on how to use Velcro to get your workspace organized:

- ☑ **Use Velcro to stick routers and cable modems and the like to the sides of furniture instead of being in the way.** This photo here is of a router fastened to the side of a desk.

✓ **Use Velcro for fastening remote controls**, especially lesser-used remotes, underneath or behind furniture.

✓ **Use Velcro for rubber stamps next to the printer.** (Stamps like "FAXED" or "COPY" or "SCANNED")

✓ **Use Velcro strips for managing cords and cables.** If you don't mind the color green, you can buy Velcro in a roll very cheaply at garden centers, intended for strapping up plants. Instead you can use it for wrapping cables!

✓ **Keep in mind that Velcro has a prickly side and a fuzzy side. You might not want the prickly side on your remote control where you'll be holding it!** The fuzzy side is soft and pleasant to hold and doesn't grab onto other fabrics, so be mindful of this when placing your Velcro strips.

✓ **Don't cover up any model numbers or serial numbers that might need to be referenced later.** Also make sure to place electronic items somewhere with proper ventilation and space around them to dissipate heat.

✓ **Place one side of the Velcro on the object with the adhesive backing peeled off, then attach the other side to that piece before peeling off its adhesive backing and pressing into place.** You want to make sure the two parts will exactly line up/match up after it's all done.

✓ **Use "Industrial Strength" Velcro for the best hold, and keep your unused Velcro strips out of heat or extreme temperatures so the adhesive won't fail later.** In our professional organizer tool kits we keep an assortment of strips and dots.

## Shipping

**Shipping is much easier now that you can purchase postage online.** The US Postal Service's Click-N-Ship® as well as UPS and FedEx are very easy options for anyone. You can print

postage on regular printer paper and tape it right to a box. All of these services provide free shipping boxes, and the US Postal Service will pick packages up from your front porch at no extra charge.

**If you are doing any significant amount of shipping, a scale is necessary to know how much postage to use.** You can pick one up at a warehouse store or office supply store, and having one will save you an immense amount of time over taking trips to the post office. If you don't want to bother with weighing anything, the USPS Flat Rate boxes are a good option. In general, if it fits in the box, it goes, for one price.

**For smaller envelopes and cards, you previously might have needed a postage meter.** Now you can use Stamps.com, or you can buy a Dymo LabelWriter Twin Turbo printer and use their Endicia postage service to print your own stamps. **Given the availability of free shipping boxes, along with boxes you receive from your own ordering online, it's tempting to be a box hoarder.** Break them down flat if you want to keep used boxes, and don't over-order the free supplies just because they are free. Boxes take up a lot of space in an office, especially if they are not flattened.

## Old Computer Equipment

**We often find somewhere in a home a "graveyard" of old computer equipment.** Clients often have procrastinated disposing of it because they don't know how to erase the data and they are not sure about where to take it.

**Goodwill has partnered with Dell to create an electronics recycling program called Dell Reconnect.** Visit *http://dellreconnect.com*, put in your zip code, and you'll find your nearest drop off location.

**They will wipe the hard drives and take care of disposing of and recycling the equipment responsibly.** See the website for a list of electronic items they will accept.

## Greener & More Efficient Printing

When you organize your printing area, a printer cart is ideal. The cart holds the printer on top and has lots of storage for supplies beneath. If your printer has wireless capability, you can locate it away from your main work surface to save space.

If you don't have a cart, look for a printer stand at office supply stores. Your printer will be raised above the work surface so that storage is available underneath, where you can store extra paper or other supplies.

For paper, have two stackable paper trays, one with printer paper (preferably recycled paper) and the other for scratch paper (those sheets printed with only one line on them and others you don't mind using).

As we mentioned in our special Velcro section, you can attach a stamp for "FAXED" or "SCANNED" or "COPY" to the side of the printer with a small Velcro dot.
**To save ink (and money!), you can set your computer's printer default settings to "Draft" mode,** which prints more lightly, and change this setting when you need to print something for more formal purposes.

**Make your printer friendlier by printing out labels to explain in your own words how to feed paper through.** Labels such as "Print Side Down, Facing Forward" and "Face Up" are much better than trying to decipher those cryptic paper feed symbols that you can never quite understand when you need a quick answer.

## Phones

**Few things will provide you with more productivity for your investment than having a headset for your land line phone!** The best selection I have found, especially for cordless rechargeable types, is at *HelloDirect.com*, but you can go to any office supply store and find corded options for around $25 or less. You can have meetings while folding laundry, cooking dinner, or typing meeting notes. It's so liberating!

**Having a speakerphone feature is also extremely helpful** to listen to conference calls and teleclasses and other things that don't require your full and undivided attention. Speakerphones are also important if more than one person in the room needs to participate in a call with others.

**Do you work with others virtually who need to be part of your company's phone system?** If you want a very professional-sounding, extremely versatile and powerful phone system for little money, use *RingCentral.com*. We have used this service for quite some time now. You can port in any number you currently use as the primary one for your business, and callers will hear a greeting of your choice that allows them a menu of selections—press 1 for customer service, press 2 to order, etc. They can also press a direct extension for someone. When the customer makes a selection, the call is sent wherever you want it—to your mobile phone, your mother-in-law's house, or your cabin in the woods. You can even transfer a live call to someone else's extension, meaning your assistant can work at her home and you from yours, and it all sounds like you are in the same office space working together.

**Consider noise and privacy needs.** Will you spend a lot of time on the phone with prospects or clients? You will need to make sure that unprofessional sounds (such as dogs barking and children crying) do not interfere with your ability to hear or talk on the phone. If you are discussing sensitive issues, you may not want others in your home to hear your conversations. This problem may need to be addressed with soundproofing or a white noise machine.

**Who is going to answer your business line?** Make sure that family members know the proper procedures for answering (or not answering!) your phone. It's usually best to leave your family members out of the process with a separate phone line and a reliable voice mail system. The way your phone is answered can have a huge bearing on your company image.

## Home-Based Businesses

Part-time, home-based business opportunities are everywhere, especially with direct selling companies

like Mary Kay, Arbonne, and Pampered Chef. I have helped clients who run these kinds of businesses, some on a small scale just beginning, and some managing large organizations.

Whether my clients have joined one of these organizations or have started their own small businesses, **I will not soon forget the products, books, and other inventory I have seen taking over homes in every available closet, cubby, and cabinet.**

**Based on these experiences, here are some questions to ask before starting a business:**

- ✓ **Does the business you intend to start involve physical inventory?**
- ✓ **If so, is there a commitment to regularly order this inventory?** You may have clear goals to be a top salesperson, but what if you're not?
- ✓ **If this inventory stacks up, where will it go?** Have a respectful conversation with your spouse/partner about the boundaries that he or she envisions for the inventory space in the garage and closets and spare rooms.
- ✓ **Have you built in a profit margin for your products that is large enough to include the cost of outsourcing the order packaging and shipping** when it gets too large for you to handle alone?
- ✓ **What are the storage needs, aside from inventory, that your business will create, such as records retention or other bulky items like books and binders?** Think about a plan for records retention with an offsite records management company if the files are really crucial—I have seen a lot of important documents in attics and basements being exposed to extreme temperatures and moisture.
- ✓ **Are there systems that colleagues are using, like accounting and sales applications that already work well in your industry?** Don't reinvent the wheel—invest in those systems up front if you are serious. In the case of network-marketing companies, there is often software or an online sales and inventory management service that makes everything work more smoothly-- USE THESE right away instead of creating your own system.
- ✓ **Do you have a designated workspace for yourself, or are you starting on a kitchen table?** Work hard to figure out a separate workspace somewhere and avoid disrupting your family's normal functions with your work materials. See our section on Finding Space also in this chapter.
- ✓ **If you already have a home-based business—is it really an active business, or is it dormant? I have seen people keeping a lot of business-related clutter around**

because they cannot admit to themselves that their business did not succeed. Having the clutter makes it feel like there is still a possibility the business could be revived... Finally admitting that the business is over frees a lot of mental energy and physical space that allows you to step forward into your next venture. Get real with yourself, mourn the loss, get support, and be brave!

## Business Visitors

**Will you be receiving visitors in your home as part of your business?** Professionals with businesses like counselors and massage therapists could have some of these issues. If so, these questions may spark a few thoughts for you that will make both the visitors and your family members more comfortable.

- **Can you hear the doorbell from your office when deliveries and visitors arrive?** Consider a doorbell extender chime, which you can purchase at a hardware store.
- **Have you checked with your city and neighborhood association for related ordinances regarding parking and hours, or even separate business entrances?** Will you need to consider additional parking? Depending upon the volume of visitors you're expecting, your business may be in violation and could be annoying your neighbors.
- **Is there adequate soundproofing and privacy for your business conversations to occur if your family is home?** You may need a white noise machine or additional insulation.
- **Will others need to let themselves into your home?** If certain people need to come and go, install a keypad garage door opener instead of distributing keys to your doors.
- **Will people need a place to sit and wait?** Make sure there is a comfortable place for waiting where evidence of your family life is not distracting.
- **What path will visitors take through your home?** What restroom will they use? Will they need to eat or cook in your kitchen or use your refrigerator?
- **Where will visitors hang coats and keep their belongings?**

## *Finding Space At Home*

**Ideally, a spare bedroom or even a dedicated study is perfect for a home office, but this is not always possible.**

**Does your formal living or dining room get used for any actual formal living and dining?** Most people don't do a lot of entertaining that requires this space. Could you add French doors or a screened partition to one of these underutilized areas and make it into an office instead?

**Many an amazing business has begun from a kitchen table.** If you must do work there, I have some strategies in a video on our tutorials page that will help (*clutterdiet.com/homeofficevideos*).

**If you don't have room for a large desk or need to save some money, a simple square card table with cover can be very adequate and still look stylish in your home.** Tablevogue makes beautiful covers for standard utility tables, and you can use the ever-versatile Elfa® file cart from the Container Store for file and drawer space, hiding it underneath the tablecloth when you need it out of sight.

**The ideal workspace is one where you can close the door when your working hours are over.** If you don't have a door, or your office is sharing space with another function in the same room, screens and other partitions are fantastic. They can subdivide larger spaces and provide some privacy. A larger living room can be partitioned with a large bookshelf unit that divides the space from a desk area. An open room that needs a door can have a screen providing that separation.

**You may need to use your own bedroom for an office, and that can work, but be careful as you may be very challenged separating your work life and personal life.** (If you are into Feng Shui, those experts say you should never do this!) If possible, relocate your office space elsewhere, and if you must, use a partition of some kind to "close up shop" and make the workspace disappear when it's time to relax.

## *Sharing Space with Your Family*

**Does your family have a separate space for their own home office and school work needs?** It's better to have duplicate sets of supplies like staplers, scissors, and tape for your business to use vs. the kids borrowing yours all the time. Ideally having a separate computer is also wise-- consider buying an older laptop for children to use instead of yours. You really don't want juice spilled all over your keyboard.

**Have you considered child care needs?** Mothers often think they can work easily while the kids nap, but it is harder than you might think. Consider trading child care favors with a friend who also works from home to provide longer windows of uninterrupted work time. Strongly consider making child care arrangements during your working hours. Make sure your children understand that the sitter is in charge—don't undermine her authority by vetoing her decisions when the children protest and complain to you. Participating in the daily decisions of the sitter will set a precedent that will cause you to be constantly interrupted to make "judgments." It is hard for children to understand that you are there but you are NOT there. Make sure the rules are clearly understood and enforced to make things less confusing for them.

**Ask yourself, "What will happen if the business really takes off?"** If you intend to work part-time only, would full-time ever work for your family if there were an incredible opportunity?

**Have an Elsewhere Basket.** You will inevitably end up with items that belong elsewhere in your house—especially if you bring in snacks from the kitchen or you have children leaving socks and toys around. Have a basket in your work area to place these items when you find them, and distribute them back to their rightful places when your workday is over.

We've covered a lot of ground here! Our next chapter shows you how to get help if you want more resources.

# GET HELP

Personal change requires three things: **Education, Motivation, and Support.**

Reading this book and watching the videos has provided you Education, and Motivation comes from your "WHY."

**But Support is the missing link in almost all efforts of change...** it's why people fall off the wagon, resume smoking, stop the diet, and quit their exercise programs. If you have someone to help you get it done, someone to be accountable to, and a cheerleader to encourage you to keep going, your chances of success go way up! Consider this:

**According to the American Society of Training and Development, the probability of completing a goal is:**

10% if you hear an idea
25% if you consciously decide to adopt it
40% if you decide when you will do it
50% if you plan how you will do it
65% if you commit to someone else you will do it
**95% if you have a specific accountability appointment
with the person to whom you committed**

**One of the best ways you can ensure your success is to find an Accountability Partner of your own.** You can call this a "Motivation Partner" if that is more your style, or even an "Organizing Buddy"—whatever makes you happy! This person can live in the same town and work with you side-by-side, trading favors getting each other's projects done, or you can check in with someone from anywhere online or on the phone. Watch the video I made for you on your bonus tutorials page at *clutterdiet.com/homeofficevideos* for particulars on choosing and working with Accountability Partners.

**Our program at ClutterDiet.com has been helping thousands of people in 18 countries since 2006 doing just that.** We are the affordable alternative to hiring a Professional

Organizer in person. Not only does our team provide you direct, personal accountability and encouragement 7 days a week in our member message board area, they also are some of the best organizing professionals in the country providing YOU their expertise on your projects!

No kidding, our memberships cost about the price of a pizza each month, and I encourage you to try our Quickstart program for FREE for 14 days.

**For help in person, go to** *www.NAPO.net,* where you can put in your zip code and find organizing professionals in your area. Look for someone who is experienced, ideally a CPO® (Certified Professional Organizer®) like those on our Clutter Diet team.

**For chronic disorganization issues, hoarding, and special needs** like brain injuries or other physical problems, the Institute for Challenging Disorganization is the best resource. **http://chronicdisorganization.org**

**Write to us and let us know how you enjoyed the book, and let us know if you have any problems or questions we can solve for you about the book itself.** You can reach us at *service@clutterdiet.com.*

**For organizing questions, please get consulting from our team at ClutterDiet.com**--again, unlimited personal help online from our expert team, free for 14 days and only $17.95 month-to-month.

It has been my pleasure to serve you with this information! **Here's hoping your time, information, and workspace is well-in-hand.**

With gratitude,

# ACKNOWLEDGEMENTS

To my clients, who provided me with immense learning experiences and enriching friendships. Thank you for our work together!

To my family, for their immense support and cheerleading and love. Thank you for tolerating my big adventure. I love you.

To my right-hand gal, Brandi ("Dolores!"). You are not only the best assistant I can imagine, you are a loyal friend. I am very grateful. And with Byron, I got a two-for-one deal! Thank you, Byron, for your friendship and your gallant help with my technology.

To the Clutter Diet Team, for providing our members with a supportive and encouraging community and being the BEST organizers in the business! Thank you for allowing me to never, ever worry that our members are in good hands.

To Susan and Audrey, for holding me accountable to actually implement all of my crazy ideas, and for listening and supporting me through all of the life stages and career ups and downs over these many years. Look at us now, wow!

To Anne ("LMF"), for continuing to think big and having great ideas, and for always being excited with me about what's happening. We have done so much together and had so much fun, and I look forward to many more years to come!

To my friend Jeffrey, for believing in my business and being so generous to help us whenever we need it. Thank you for your consistent presence, your impressive brain, and your unwavering support.

To Kendra Cagle, for the great job on our cover and the other projects you've been doing for us this year. You're wonderful!

To Brendon Burchard, my mentor, who has challenged me and inspired me for many years. Thank you for raising the bar for the expert industry and for all of the opportunities you've brought my way. "I'm here!" And I am living, loving, and mattering.

# ABOUT THE AUTHOR

Certified Professional Organizer® Lorie Marrero is the bestselling author of *The Clutter Diet®: The Skinny on Organizing Your Home and Taking Control of Your Life*. She is also the creator of ClutterDiet.com, an innovative program allowing anyone to get expert help at an affordable price since 2006.

Her organizing books and products are sold online and in stores nationwide, including her Simple Division® Garment Organizers, available at The Container Store®. This product is proudly assembled with care by people with disabilities and disadvantages who are employed at Goodwill Industries.®

Lorie is the spokesperson for Goodwill Industries International, and she is a sought-after expert for national media such as CNBC, *Family Circle*, WGN News and *Woman's Day*. She has also served as a spokesperson for many other companies, including Staples, Brother, Swingline, and Microsoft, and she writes frequently as an organizing expert for *Good Housekeeping*.

She lives an ecstatically happy life in Austin, TX with her human family and 30,000 bee daughters in her very own beehives.

Get free tips & videos @ www.clutterdiet.com/freetips

 Clutter Diet Blog
www.clutterdietblog.com

 Clutter Diet Program
www.clutterdiet.com

 Facebook
www.facebook.com/clutterdiet

 Google+
http://gplus.to/loriemarrero

 Instagram
www.instagram.com/loriemarrero

 Pinterest
www.pinterest.com/loriemarrero

 Twitter
www.twitter.com/clutterdiet

 YouTube
www.clutterdiet.tv

### Hire Lorie as a speaker!

Contact us at service@clutterdiet.com or 866-915-3438 ext. 71
to discuss your organization's needs.

CPSIA information can be obtained at www.ICGtesting.com
Printed in the USA
LVOW02s1553120813

347503LV00001B/23/P

9 780982 609026